A GLIMPSE OF AMERICA
and other Lectures, Interviews and Essays

Bram Stoker's
A GLIMPSE of AMERICA

and other Lectures, Interviews and Essays

Edited and Introduced by
Richard Dalby

Series Editor: Clive Leatherdale

Desert Island Books

First Published in 2002 by
DESERT ISLAND BOOKS LIMITED
7 Clarence Road, Southend-on-Sea, Essex SS1 1AN
United Kingdom
www.desertislandbooks.com

British Library Cataloguing-in-Publication Data
A catalogue record for this book is available from the British Library

ISBN 1-874287-35-X

Printed in Great Britain by
4Edge Ltd

Donation checked by: _NR_____

Year of Publication   2002

Available at:

	Yes/No	# of copies
Education Library	No	
Orillia Education		
Chancellor Paterson Library		
Harvie Legacy		
Law Library		
Other LU Library		

Other Editions Available (Please specify year and library):

Better World Books wants it ☒

Better World books does not want it ☐

Contents

Introduction

Bram Stoker's reputation as the author of *Dracula* and other sensational novels has always overshadowed his parallel literary career as a journalist and lecturer.

The biographies by Harry Ludlam (1962), Daniel Farson (1975) and Barbara Belford (1996) have given only tantalisingly brief references and quotations from Stoker's fascinating and controversial articles like 'The Question of a National Theatre', and 'The Censorship of Fiction', but they have never been fully collected and reprinted in their entirety for modern readers and scholars.

Stoker's first important public lecture (or 'address') on 'The Necessity for Political Honesty' was delivered in the dining hall of Trinity College at Dublin on 13 November 1872, and immediately published as a cheap paperback by James Charles & Son, thereby becoming the writer's first official (and now rarest) publication, seven years before *The Duties of Clerks of Petty Sessions in Ireland* (1879).

Almost equally rare, and highly sought after by Stoker collectors, is another ephemeral booklet, *A Glimpse of America*, the complete text of a lecture given at the London Institution on 28 December 1885, published by Sampson Low in early 1886.

This lively account of the New World was composed after Stoker's tour there with Henry Irving and the Lyceum Theatre Company from November 1884 to April 1885. The explorer H.M. Stanley told Irving that Stoker's lecture 'had in it more information about America than any other book that had ever been written', while the American poet James Whitcomb Riley declared: 'Good! Splendid! Keen! Sharp! Observant! Superb!' The *Pall Mall Gazette* praised Stoker for his 'keen eye for humorous touches', adding that 'the salient and distinctive points of American life' had been 'so accurately stated'.

Stoker's early years as an unpaid, anonymous theatre critic in Dublin formed invaluable experience for his later journalism in London. During his 26 years with Irving (1879-1905), most of his articles were directly connected with the theatre, notably 'Actor-Managers' (1890; published in conjunction with two shorter pieces by Henry Irving and Charles Wyndham), 'Dramatic Criticism' (1894) and 'The Art of Ellen Terry' (1901).

These articles and essays were really extended lectures in all but name, and it is easy to picture the flamboyant red-bearded Irishman proclaiming them from a stage to captivated audiences.

After Irving's death in 1905, and the publication of Stoker's two-volume biography *Personal Reminiscences of Henry Irving,* (1906), Bram

– despite his failing health – concentrated on full-time journalism and the writing of fiction. The *World's Work* magazine commissioned him to write two pieces for their special Irish number in May 1907 on 'The Great White Fair in Dublin' and 'The World's Greatest Shipbuilding Yard'.

He was also a regular contributor to some of the most prominent literary and political journals of the era, including *The Nineteenth Century and After* and *The Fortnightly Review*, two of the leading progressive organs for the Victorian and Edwardian intelligentsia. Six of Stoker's important articles and essays in these two journals appear in the present volume.

Stoker continued to enlighten his readers on many different aspects of the theatre, notably the ever-growing number of 'Dead-heads' (or non-paying guests), which managers had to contend with every day. The vast number of letters written to Stoker, now housed in the Brotherton Collection at Leeds University, include many hundreds of requests from his innumerable acquaintances applying for gratis Lyceum tickets. It is estimated that Stoker may have written up to one thousand short notes and letters each week (or one million over 26 years) dealing with all aspects of the Lyceum management.

He always greatly admired the energy, determination and technique of 'Americans as Actors', finding that they only lacked experience.

Back in the 1880s, Stoker somehow found time to resume his serious studies for the Bar, having drafted the rules for the Actors' Benevolent Fund and various societies in London. He was called to the Bar, Inner Temple, in his 43rd year, shortly before writing his treatise on 'Actor-Managers'.

Stoker's keen interest in the law and medieval legal history is clearly demonstrated in several of his learned articles, notably 'The American Tramp Question'. He wrote extensively on the timeless problems of vagrancy and the 'bone-idle', suggesting that persistent vagrants and unemployed people should be indelibly marked (rather than violently branded), taken to labour colonies and taught intensively how to work.

During my researches for Bram Stoker's *Bibliography* in 1982, I was delighted to discover for the first time a series of profiles and interviews with some of his notable friends in 1907 and 1908 – Arthur Conan Doyle, W.S. Gilbert, Arthur Wing Pinero and a young Winston S. Churchill in the year of his marriage. These were printed in London's *Daily Chronicle* and the New York *World* – and it is possible that several other Stoker profiles and articles may still lie there undetected.

These fascinating conversations bring not only his subjects but also Stoker himself to life more than any other of his writings after the

Personal Reminiscences of Henry Irving. It is to be regretted that no journalist of this period interviewed Stoker in equal depth.

Collecting all these profiles, essays, articles and lectures together in book form has always been a long-held ambition of mine, and I am now extremely gratified – with the invaluable help of William Hughes, Alan Johnson and Clive Leatherdale – that Desert Island Books is now including this volume in the Dracula Library of rare Stoker works, coinciding with the 90th anniversary of his death on 20 April 1912 at 26 St. George's Square, London.

Richard Dalby
Scarborough, April 2002

Richard Dalby, a freelance writer, editor, bibliographer and antiquarian bookseller, has been collecting gothic literature and the works of Bram Stoker for more than thirty years. He compiled *Bram Stoker: A Bibliography of First Editions* (1983), and has discovered and reprinted hundreds of supernatural tales (in addition to many new stories) in several anthologies including *Dracula's Brood* (1987), *Vampire Stories* (1992), and *The Mammoth Book of Victorian and Edwardian Ghost Stories* (1995). He has also edited numerous single-author collections including S. Baring-Gould's long-forgotten vampire novella *Margery of Quether and other Weird Tales* (1999), and co-edited *The Best Ghost and Horror Stories of Bram Stoker* for Dover in 1997. He unearthed and introduced Stoker's rare first novel *The Primrose Path* (1875) for the Desert Island Dracula Library in 1999.

PART 1

Lectures

A Glimpse of America

'After all there's a great deal of human nature in man.' This conclusion of the great humorist is probably that of every traveller, whose only experiences or impressions of any general interest are those which show the minor developments of human instincts in new surroundings, and under new conditions. We Londoners have opportunities of witnessing, in our daily life, the whole scheme of human existence. We have points of contact with as high a civilisation as the earth affords; and also, I fear, with here and there, as complete a system of savagery as distinguished those aborigines who won a place in history by resting on the outside of Captain Cook. Being cognisant, therefore, of the zenith and the nadir of the star of human progress, and knowing the ultimate limits of which our nature is capable, we must not expect to find in other places, and amongst other peoples, any very startling divergence from our own principles of action, or from the consequences which follow them. I may say, at the outset of my remarks, that I shall not try to convey such crude thoughts as spring from personal comfort or discomfort in strange places and new situations, but shall try to make known the results of the study of points to which my attention was called, consciously or unconsciously, by the incidents of changing life, or from the understanding of conditions of existence new to me. I shall be your eyes and ears in matters on which I found myself ignorant; but shall try to be so with a larger knowledge than I formerly possessed. In fact, I shall ask you to come with my memory, rather than to follow my exact footsteps through a journey in a new land. I shall notice only points of difference, for the similarities are million-fold.

The first impression of America which an average Englishman will experience, will probably be on losing sight of his own shore, and will be one of very great ignorance of the country which he is about to visit.

It is to me, having once visited America, deplorable that we can be left so ignorant of a nation, not merely like ourselves, but ourselves – the same in blood, religion, and social ideas, with an almost identical common law, and with whom our manifold interests are not only vast, but almost vital. I really doubt if the average educated Briton could tell how many States or Territories are in the American Union, the extent of the population, or of the space they spread over, or of the practical conditions under which they live. Such matters as the difference between a State and a Territory, or between National law and State law, are known only to a comparative few, and to the vast majority of us our want of knowledge of the principles and conditions of the executive is ignorance carried to a positive quality. In some ways this ignorance of ours is not only an individual loss, but a national misfortune. The value to us of a widespread and accurate knowledge of a country with which we have so much to do in the way of business, and whose ramifications on lines similar to our own are so vast, is simply immeasurable. A country which contains, in a pretty solid square, lying mainly between the 30 and 50 parallels of North latitude, an area of 3,611,689 square miles, with a population, in 1880, of 50,152,866, with colleges, schools, and asylums to the number of 141,629, with (in 1884) 124,281 miles of railroad, and with 11,403 newspapers and periodicals.

Such figures as these do not, perhaps, carry any distinct idea by themselves, but they may be popularly explained by comparison with home statistics. For instance, New York is nearly as far from San Francisco as from London. While our largest county – Yorkshire – contains 3,882,851 acres, Texas, the largest of the 38 States of the Union, has 170,099,200 acres. Roughly, Texas is as large as France, with Holland, Belgium, Denmark, and Greece thrown in, and the scale nicely balanced with the West Riding of Yorkshire. In this vast dominion is a population (in 1880) of 1,591,740, about the same as that of the county of Surrey.

I am anxious that we should have some sort of idea of these things, so that at the start we may get a general idea of the importance to this country of a knowledge of a great community, where every little matter of business or sentiment which can be between two people is multiplied fifty million-fold, so that the drops of individual interest swell into a mighty torrent of good or ill.

I shall try to speak of America as it struck me, in two respects – social and political. I speak entirely without prejudice, and I give a thought simply because it came to me somehow or from some cause.

The social conditions of American life are of peculiar interest, for in them may be seen by a strange eye, not already jaundiced by prejudice, distinct methods of race development. Naturally life is more or less regulated by the material conditions of its surroundings. A country which, at its centre of population, has a temperature varying from 20 degrees below zero to 100 above it, must be subject to conditions of social life not possible in more equal temperatures. There are in the United States places where the temperature is equable; but, in the average, there are degrees of heat in summer and cold in winter to which we are strangers. Thus, every arrangement of domestic economy must be made duplicate, to contend opposite evils of heat and cold. To protect life, as well as to ensure comfort, in winter-time every door and window must be capable of being closed hermetically; and to make life bearable in the summer-time there must be cool verandahs and generously-opened doorways, where the burning sunshine cannot penetrate, even by reflection.

The centre of population, as defined formally, is 'the point at which equilibrium would be reached, were the country taken as a plane surface, itself without weight, but capable of sustaining weight, and loaded with its inhabitants, in number and position as they are found at the period under consideration, each individual being assumed to be of the same specific gravity as every other, and, consequently, to exert pressure on the pivotal point directly proportioned to his distance therefrom.'

The centre of population is, by the Census of 1880 – the latest taken – fixed a few miles from Cincinnati, in the State of Ohio. Here, though in summer the temperature rises to 100 Fahrenheit, two winters ago the ground whilst I was there was frozen six feet deep, and from the thaw along the watershed of the Ohio River the whole country was becoming inundated. The day we left the city the water was rushing over the levees, as they call the banks built to protect the lower lands. A few days later the water had risen to a height of 60 feet over its normal level. The terrible severity of the winters thus often changes abnormally the whole conditions of life. The recurrence of climatic disasters makes a new danger in ordinary life. In cities where the winter is severe, and especially in those of new growth, the imperfect nature of the roadways, and the difficulty of keeping them open, at times renders private traffic difficult and expensive, and tends in part to explain the immense use made all through America of tramcars and public stages of all kinds. With us persons of a certain class think it *infra dignatate* to ride in tramcars, as also to wear overshoes, or to wrap up against the weather; in all these things Americans are quite free, and do not hesitate to do as they think best. In winter no one dreams of going without overshoes or arctics – boots to cover ordinary boots, made of felt and india-rubber. I have often admired the dexterity and completeness with which all American ladies protect themselves and their clothes from the weather. Overshoes for the feet, a long circular mackintosh reaching almost to the ground, and a veil woven round the hat and covering the face, renders them proof against rain or snow.

The extent of the country has a distinct effect on social life, as it renders long journeys frequent and short journeys necessary. Nothing brings home to me the influence of distances on life so strongly as the way in which the word 'road' has come to have a special meaning. With us a road is a carriage-road – 'the King's highway,' as it used to be called – and when we apply it to special purposes we give it a qualifying distinction, such as *rail*road; but in America, where vast distances are opened up by railway enterprise, and where, except in the towns, there are but few roads, as we know them, the word 'road' is applied, not by written authority, but by common use to railways, without any qualifying prefix. We hear, with us, of the London Road, the York Road, &c. In America we know the Burlington Road, the Erie

Road, &c. It is, perhaps, not so odd that this should be so, when we consider that whilst in the United Kingdom we had, in 1884, all told, 18,864 miles of railway, the mileage of the United States was 124,281.

A further evidence of the change with regard to highways is that, although American social ideas, habits, and traditions are, in the main, English, our rule of the road is there reversed, and riders and drivers keep the off, or right-hand, side.

An important factor of social change is the inadequacy of domestic service. In a country where a few years of successful toil or enterprise often realises wealth, there is naturally a desire for workers to seek the most remunerative employment. This is not to be found under the average conditions of household work. Consequent on the scarcity and expense of domestic service, social routine and social appliances are formulated to the simplest possible plan. In fact, the great system of immense residential hotels is a natural growth. These hotels are to be found in every city of the Union. Some of them are of vast extent, being able to supply accommodation for 800 or 1,000 persons. Some of the seaside hotels are of fabulous extent. I believe that in Coney Island, near New York, there are hotels where 10,000 persons can put up. One of these is pointed out as being an example – perhaps the only one – of a building so large as to be able to exemplify with its rooftree, duly levelled, the curvature of the earth's surface.

For the same reason, the system of houses apportioned in flats, with a common kitchen, and often a common service, have multiplied to a great degree. All through America the major part of domestic service is undertaken by Irish and Negroes, with here and there Germans and Italians, the latter chiefly in restaurants, of which in every city there is a large number. Up to the present time in the United States, domestic service has been regarded as one of the lower orders of work, and it was only within my own experience of the country, beginning in the autumn of 1883, that liveries were to be seen, except at rare intervals, even with carriage servants. I have, several times, heard the fact loudly deplored by Americans, who looked on it as a sign of the waning of that spirit of independence which has hitherto characterised the citizens of the country. Domestic service, and its kindred employment, the police, seem excellently paid, in so far as wages go. In most of the big cities female servants get from £40 to £50 sterling wages, besides excellent living and proper bedrooms, and a much larger measure of personal freedom than at home we are willing to allow. Policemen get large wages, partly, perhaps, due to the fact that they are generally ward politicians. In New York their pay is about, on the average, $100 per month, or £240 *per annum*, out of which they have to find their own clothes, which are of the best. I may here remark that all through America men and women of the working classes are much better dressed than at home, and this under the penalising condition of an import *ad valorem* duty running in cotton from 35 to 50 per cent, in silk 50 per cent all round, and in woollen from 45 per cent in the yarn to 90 per cent in the piece, and when made into clothing 67 per cent.

A traveller, going through the country in the ordinary way, by railways, steamboats, stages, and road-cars, could not possibly distinguish classes as at home, except when they are of very marked difference, or, of course, in the case of tramps, and other excretions of civilisation.

The tramp is, in America, a class by himself, tolerated simply for the time. In the vast population of the country there is, of course, a percentage of incurable drones; their number is not many, but they form a dangerous element, since they have no home, and are without the responsibilities which regulate in some degree their fellows; consequently, they are at times treated with ruthless severity, when, for instance, some outrage has been committed, particularly when a woman has been the victim. In the latter instance, when a negro has been the delinquent, he is almost invariably lynched. In some communities, tramps are warned off, and threatened with being 'shot on sight,' a summary process of the social law not holding a place in our code.

It is, of course, in the towns that social life is most regulated by conventional standards. America, except in few instances, has not those vast country houses which are studded throughout the Old World. The old order of things of the plantation and slavery period has changed, and the new manifestations of the aristocracy of wealth have not yet been completed. In and around Boston, Philadelphia, New York, and Baltimore are great houses; but the rule, even in the cases of the wealthiest people, is to have more moderate establishments than would be found with the owners of equal wealth at home. Certainly they have every conceivable comfort and luxury, when such are attainable. Every man builds his own house accordingly to his own wants. The consequence is a general picturesque effect, and the creation of almost a new order of domestic architecture. The American architects are well to the fore, and with the experience of the Old World, and the opportunities of the New, can almost, in the routine of their daily work, indulge their creative artistic tastes. Such men as Richardson, of Boston, and Stanford White, of New York, are doing work which shall be, in a large measure, a memorial of their age. In the United States are many houses of striking beauty, and many streets where the majority of houses are good, with some notable examples of sound artistic work. Such, for instance, are Beacon Street, Boston, Prairie and Michigan Avenues, Chicago, and North Avenue, Buffalo. Some of the houses in New York are also of great beauty.

The clubs form a very distinct portion of social life. Every city has several. They are, as a rule, large, handsome, and excellently appointed.

Their hospitality is unbounded, and the stranger who is properly introduced is made a member for the necessary time with a facility and rapidity which is impossible amongst our denser population. The club in America is, indeed, to the masculine wayfarer the shadow of a great rock in a long and thirsty land. I often felt chagrin at the thought that we English can never repay in any similar way this expression of American hospitality.

Nearly every one of moderate means has some country or seaside residence. It may be small, but is the absolute possession of the owner, and is at present easily obtainable. I have known a player in the orchestra of a theatre who had his cottage in the country, bought with and supported by his own savings. This possession of real estate is in every way fostered and encouraged by the policy of the United States. Land is supposed to be held for useful purposes, and its transfer is exceedingly cheap and simple. A few hours and a few dollars can transfer a whole estate.

In his message to Congress on the 8th of December, 1885, President Cleveland crystallised into a few sentences the public feeling with regard to land: 'It is not,' he said, 'for the common benefit of the United States that a large area of the public land should be acquired, directly, or through fraud, into the hands of a single individual. As far as practicable the plan adopted in the disposal of the public lands should have in view the original policy, which encouraged many pur-chasers of these lands for homes, and discouraged the massing of large areas.'

This was said with reference to the Public Domain, which is the great reserve of lands in various parcels, disposable, as thought desir-able, by the Federal Government of the United States; but of course such a public policy was the outcome of public needs, and of the expe-rience of individuals and of controlling local powers, and may, there-fore, be taken as evidence of the existing public sentiment.

The habit and facility, then, of acquiring freehold encourages the building everywhere of residences for personal use, and affects, not only the design of the house, but the quality of the labour and the material used. It seemed to me that everywhere the constructive work is admirably done. The work of the stonemasons is really sound and good, and the plumbing is of the best. Work of each of these kinds is expensive, the latter specially so. They have a caustic saying in some places, that if you get the plumbers into your house, even for repairs, it is better for you to offer the entire freehold in liquidation of the debt rather than to undertake to pay the bill.

Amongst the conveniences and facilities of life, springing from the highly-developed organisation of a limited supply of service, I may mention the fire brigade. In America fire brigades are even more nec-essary than with us, partly because there are still so many wooden houses, and partly because there is a special danger arising from the necessity of indoor warmth. Where the cold is intense it is necessary to maintain much heat within doors, a practice, by the way, which, to our differently-schooled powers of sensation, seems overdone at times.

In New York and some other places a system of steam-pipes has been laid through some streets, so that participants can take in, as we do our gas, whatever amount of pressure as may be required, and regulate it accordingly, a practice which minimises danger of fire.

All over the Union the fire brigades are admirable. I do not know anything more inspiriting than to see them work, for the whole force seems everywhere animated by a superb ardour. In New York, Chicago, and I believe San Francisco, the way in which the work is done is quite wonderful. Each city is divided into sections, all communicating with each other. Day and night the staff on duty is ready for instant work.

Let me describe a fire station and its working: It is night; everything is still. The main room of the station is separated from the street by great gates, now shut. In front of the gate as you enter is a large wagon, piled with ladders and all the implements necessary for raising them in the fewest seconds possible. Behind is a fire-engine. A little way back, on each side, are horses tethered in stalls. From the sides of the room brass poles, two inches thick, rise up through circular openings in the ceiling, some three or four feet across, to the room above. One man is writing in a little railed-in desk. No one else is visible. The firemen are asleep in their beds upstairs.

An electric gong sounds.

In a single second everything is changed. The place becomes instinct with life and action. The same mechanism which strikes the gong releases the horses, who rush into the shafts of the ladder-wagon. The men overhead, waked by the gong, jump from their beds into their big boots, which stand by ready, and actually throw themselves into the room below, sliding down the brass rods. They jump on the escape, where their coats and helmets hang ready for them. The harness of the horses is suspended by strings from the ceilings. One snap of a buckle on the collar of each, and the harnessing is done. The action of taking the reins detaches the supporting strings, which are counterweighted and disappear; the gates fly open, and, fully manned and equipped, the rescuing escape rushes on its way.

It is almost incredible till one sees it done; but commonly, seven seconds after the gong has sounded, the fire-escape is at full gallop in the street. The time sometimes is diminished so low as four seconds. Just fancy the value of every second when life is at stake. The men, and even the horses, seem to understand and act.

The fire-engines, too, get out with marvellous rapidity. In the cellars of the station are fixed boilers, in connection with the engines,

which are kept filled with boiling water at high pressure. The movement of the engine from its place, by an automatic contrivance, cuts off
the connection and lights the fire of the boiler, so as to keep up the
existing pressure of steam.

Finest of all appliances in this special service is what they call the
'Hook and Ladder Company,' of which there is one in every station.
This is a recent development, and is most successful in saving life in
extreme cases. Individual heroism is the active force. There are a number of short ladders, some ten feet long, very light – a single shaft, with
crescent-shaped foot-pieces screwed on, and a steel hook at the top,
some four feet long, fixed at right angles and serrated on the inside, so
as to lay hold of any projection, however small or large. On the outside, at the top, is a small hook, and the fireman has a strong ring in
his belt, into which it can be fixed. The company work as follows:
From the footpath the fireman holding the latter by the foot throws the
hook through the window above, where it catches on the inner edge of
the wall. He then runs up the ladder, fixes the ring at his belt in the
hook, and is able, with the leverage given by leaning out, to attach a
similar ladder, handed to him from below, to the window of the next
storey. To this ladder comes another fireman, and so, storey by storey,
up they go, a perpetually ascending stream of men and ladders, till
they reach the point at which they aim.

Two years ago a case occurred which stamped itself upon my own
memory. At the top of a block of residential flats, as high as the Queen
Anne's Mansions, a boy was left during a fire. All escape was cut off.
No ladder could reach so high, and the stairs were blocked with smoke
and flame.

To the rescue the Hook and Ladder Company!

On they came – quiet, agile, resolute, and with the calm coolness
that marks the brave. Not a second was lost; for it was a race with
flame, and a life the stake. Up they swarmed, up the dizzy heights; the
crowd around them silent as death – no sound but the roaring of the
flame, the crash and sharp stroke of the engines, and the hissing of the
water on the fire. At last the roof was won, only just in time to catch
the boy as he fell fainting. You can fancy the roar of the crowd as those
heroes came with their burden down that fiery path.

At times the firemen have to work under conditions seemingly
impossible. I saw once at St. Louis a house which had been burnt in the
night, and the ruins were coated with ice where the water was frozen,
almost as it fell. In Chicago I saw the water turn to ice where it touched
the wall of a burning house in places where the flames had not yet
reached.

Amongst the minor organisations of service are the messenger
service and the signalling system. The messenger system, which exists
in nearly every American city, might, I think, be adopted with great

advantage here. Thickly studded throughout the city are offices, where there wait a number of boys in uniform, who can be sent when required at a fixed tariff for time or distance. These offices are in communication with livery establishments, and with police and fire-stations, and also with the vast majority of private dwellings – in fact, with every one who will establish a signal in his house. Thus, by ringing an electric bell in a specified manner – one pull, two, three, or four – you can summon to your house a messenger boy, a carriage, a policeman, or a fire brigade.

One of the most marked characteristics of American life is the high regard in which woman is held. It seems, now and then, as if a page of an old book of chivalry had been taken as the text of a social law. Everywhere there is the greatest deference, everywhere a protective spirit. Such a thing as a woman suffering molestation or affront, save at the hands of the criminal classes – which are the same all the world over – is almost unknown, and would be promptly resented by the first man coming along. I think I may fairly say that, from the Canadian lakes to the Gulf of Mexico, or from Sandy Hook to the Golden Gate, a woman can walk abroad as safely as she can remain at home. In some ways, the idea, which is a noble one, is carried out to a pitch which, to those not accustomed to it, seems at least extreme. Thus, for instance, with regard to banking queues. The system of the queue, formulated by the French Revolution into a habit, holds in America. Everywhere the later comer takes his place in turn. Banks, like other establishments, are, by our ideas, generally undermanned, and it is sometimes necessary to wait a little while to be able either to pay in or draw out money. Every man, of course, takes his place in turn and waits; but when a woman comes she at once heads the rank, instead of taking her place in it. A half-grown girl, or a servant-maid, will thus keep waiting, in the busiest hour of the day, men whose minutes are golden.

This protective spirit has, I fancy, much to do with the freedom which women enjoy. By freedom, I mean the relaxing of those petty restraints which, with us, are rather recollections or traditions than social needs, or a logical outcome of the spirit of the age. In the United States a young woman is, almost if not quite, as free to think and act for herself as a young man is. This personal freedom is of course based on a large measure of education, practical as well as of book-learning, and has its correlative in a very stringent law of personal discretion. I was much struck with this point in relation to suicides. There is not, that I know, any means of forming an exact estimate, but it seemed to me that of the suicides reported in the papers the vast majority were women, mostly young, and with, in every case, a sad old story behind.

It is, of course, almost impossible to make any accurate statement of the social condition of a country which shows the remarkable fact of

a whole population of fifty millions simultaneously moving to a higher social plane. The only written evidence we can have is in the books
of etiquette, which, inasmuch as they have to fulfil the requirements of
the age, record by inference its social condition. In these 'abstract and
brief chronicles,' – which are in no wise to be lightly regarded – we
find everywhere a strong measure of common sense, and the manifestations of what we might call the 'natural laws' of good manners. In
these volumes courtesy and good feeling are laid down as axioms, and
general laws are evolved. The need of such works is shown in the
changing customs of social life. Thus, for instance, in 1860, it was 'good
form' for a woman to sign herself in a letter *Mrs.* or *Miss*, and custom
then countenanced the fashion of 'presenting compliments' on formal
occasions. In 1885, we learn that the latter form 'has been discarded for
quite a number of years,' and that the former method of signature 'is
everywhere looked upon as a vulgarity.'

The natural bridge between social and political life is education;
and before we enter upon the latter domain it is well to understand the
high place which education holds as a public need. This is, perhaps,
best exemplified by the Amendment to the Constitution of the State of
Massachusetts, made in 1857 by the necessary majority of its State
Senators and two-thirds of the House of Representatives: 'No person shall
have the right to vote, or be eligible to office under the Constitution of
this Commonwealth, who shall not be able to read the Constitution in
the English language, and to write his name,' &c. It is also shown by
the 11th Amendment of the Constitution of Connecticut, in 1855,
which requires ability to read as a condition of the suffrage.

Suitable provision is made in nearly every State for public education. In the new States and Territories this is insisted on to a remarkable degree, and with excellent effects. For the purposes of public
schools, every sixteenth section of public land is set apart in the States
admitted prior to 1848, and every sixteenth and thirty-sixth section of
such land in States and Territories since organised, estimated at
1,165,520 acres. Public lands are also set aside for the purposes of sem-
inaries, universities, and agricultural and other colleges. As the public
lands are mapped out into six-mile sections, these again divided into
square miles, it can be easily understood what fine provision is made
for the educational future. The Report of the Commission of Education
for 1882-3 gives the result that out of a school population of, in the
United States, 16,243,822, no less than 10,013,826 were enrolled in public schools, the average daily attendance being 6,118,331, the average
duration of schooldays varying from 62 to 200 per annum.

I was myself much struck with the condition of education. It was
quite a delight to see now and again a lad of seventeen or eighteen
years old come into a bookshop to buy a cheap edition of an arithmetic
of the higher order, or some equally advanced work in other solid subjects.

Sometimes the amount of knowledge shown, where one does not expect it, almost gives a shock to the stranger. For instance, a hackman in Chicago, who was pointing out to me as we drove along the various buildings, showed me one which he specified as a scientific institution.

'What do they teach?' I asked.

He answered, 'Oh, every form of scientific knowledge, from pure mathematics to practical engineering!'

In a small place in the West, a journeyman printer, whom I wanted to do some work in a style somewhat unusual, said:–

'We can do it if you like, but I assure you it will not be consonant with the traditions of typographic art.'

Not only is there throughout the United States a general educational effort, but, here and there, a tendency is manifested to achieve a high grade in special knowledge. For instance, the Massachusetts Institute of Technology is a very perfect high school of scientific effort, and the John Hopkins' University of Maryland is practically creating a great school of its own, especially in comparative history.

In anything which I may say of politics, I wish it distinctly borne in mind that I use the word purely in the English, and not the American sense, and in nowise in connection with party strife. In America, the word has fallen very low, and a 'politician' – unless you hear or know to the contrary – is a man whom it is, perhaps, as well not to trust too much. I prefer to designate those persons who take an active part in the higher Administration as 'statesmen,' so as to avoid any confusion of ideas. An American once told me an incident, which as it came through such a source, I may, I hope, without offence, repeat. It was to the effect that a stranger, coming to the country in the midst of a local election, asked his host:–

'Why is it that you prefer to elect your officials from the criminal classes?'

The reason of the possibility of such a query can be better understood by anyone who has attended a 'primary' meeting, where the rowdy element asserts itself.

The Republican form of Government aims at giving freedom of every possible kind. Each sacrifice, therefore, of individual or corporate rights is made to a higher and farther-reaching power. Thus, the National Government has, within the whole area of Republican America, absolute control of the matters entrusted to it by the Constitution of the United States. In this category are all matters of National (or, as we should say, Imperial) interest – taxation and finance, coinage, the regulation of weights and measures, naturalisation, laws of bankruptcy, regulation of commerce, foreign policy, Supreme Courts, the postal system, copyright, International law, declaration of war, management of the Army, Navy, and Militia, treaties, protection of Indian tribes, &c.

All matters not specially confided to the National Congress are absolutely controlled by each State in its own way, with certain Constitutional limitations, such as absolute free trade and extradition between State and State, the guarantee of Republican form of government, and the obligation of contracts. The State, in turn, is sub-divided into Counties, which have absolute self-government in all matters not directly regulated by the Nation or the State. These, again, have sub-divisions, self-controlling for local purposes, where not regulated by higher forms of legislation.

Thus the whole structure of the Republic is cellular, and built up from entities through various minor forms and agglomerations into a compact, cohesive, and structurally perfect mass.

Like all cellular formations, it is a natural growth. Sir Henry Maine, in his recent work on 'Popular Government,' takes especial pains to show that the Constitution of the United States is not by any means original, but that it is in reality founded on the British Constitution as it existed between 1760 and 1787, modified by the study, on the part of its founders, of the ancient Republics, and the Romano-German Empire.

Mr. Freeman attributes to the fact, that *because* it was not original, as was the constitution of the French Republic founded at the same time, 'it lived on, that it has gone through the most frightful of trials, and that it abides, and promises long to abide.'

Professor Fiske declares that 'the Government of the United States is not the result of special creation, but of evolution,' and that 'the town-meeting' – the Teutonic *folkmoot* – 'lies at the bottom of all political life of the United States.'

Professor Shinn, in a recent most interesting work, shows the influence of mining laws on the development of the country, and consequently on the laws which govern it. He tells how the mining laws, evolved from the experience of miners in ancient Egypt and Phoenicia – in the period of Roman supremacy – in the Hartz Mountains and in Cornwall, were naturally revived in the great mining epoch of 1848-49, and predicts that a century hence 'the atmosphere and traditions of the mining camp will linger in the fragments of the miners' jurisprudence which will yet remain firmly embedded in local and State law.'

The impression which I think an unprejudiced Englishman must derive from a first knowledge of the American political system, is of the extraordinary perfection of its theory and the elasticity of its working. Naturally, one is more attracted by the machinery of the Federation than with the working of local institutions; and inasmuch as all, or nearly all, the State Constitutions are founded on, and are all in harmony with, the National Constitution, a brief glance at the political system may not be amiss.

There are three great departments of activity under the Constitution of the United States – the Legislative, the Executive, and the Judicial. The entire Legislative powers are vested in a Congress, consisting of a Senate and a House of Representatives. The Senate is composed of two members from each State (without regard to its size), chosen by the State Legislatures to serve for six years. Senators must be at least thirty years of age, resident in their State, and have been citizens for nine years. The elections have been, at the beginning, so arranged that every second year one-third of the Senate is renewed.

The House of Representatives is composed of members elected every second year by popular vote, the number for each State being fixed by the census taken every tenth year – every State having at least one member. By the original Constitution of 1789, the ratio of representation to population was fixed not to exceed 1 in 30,000. The enormous growth of the population is shown by the fact that, whilst the original number of representatives was 65, distributed amongst 13 States, the present representation, although the number is increased to 325, spread over 38 States, only allows of a ratio of one to each 154,325 persons.

The House of Representatives is similar to our House of Commons, and has similar powers, especially in that only with it fiscal bills can originate. The members are elected to sit each for a district of the State, as it is considered good public policy that they should be in actual touch with their constituents.

All members of Congress, Senators and Representatives alike, are paid an annual salary of $5,000, or £1,000 sterling. For this they are bound to do duty if required. Provision is made in the Constitution to enable each house to make the necessary laws to carry the idea into effect. As at present working, the Sergeant-at-Arms, at the direction of the House, can arrest absent members and compel their attendance.

The Executive power is vested in the President, elected each fourth year, and who appoints his own cabinet. He is Commander-in-Chief of the Army and Navy, has power to reprieve, appoints ambassadors and judges of the Supreme Court, and can, with the consent of the Senate, make treaties. The President must be native born, at least 35 years of age, and have resided fourteen years within the United States. His manner of election is as follows:–

To form an Electoral College, each State elects representatives to the number of their combined number of Congressmen and Senators. With this College rests the election. Practically, these representatives are chosen as delegates of the contesting political parties, and as each party, through its Convention, decides on one candidate for the Presidential chair, the election is something like a plebiscite, taken State by State.

Thus, in the political system, are several quite different methods of popular representation:–

(a) The President, chosen by a State plebiscite;

(b) The Senate, chosen by the State Legislatures; and

(c) The House of Representatives, chosen directly by district suffrage. Thus there is everywhere a check against undue influence.

It is a popular fallacy that in the United States the principle of universal suffrage holds. It does not, either in theory or in fact. The original Constitution of 1789 simply lays down that 'The electors in each State shall have the qualifications requisite for electors of the most numerous branch of the State Legislature.' How this is qualified may be seen in the Constitutions of the various States. Thus Massachusetts and Connecticut ordain an educational test. Paupers are disqualified in Delaware, Maine, New Hampshire, New Jersey, Texas, and West Virginia. Rhode Island requires a property qualification of $134. Pennsylvania, Massachusetts and Georgia exclude non-taxpayers, Tennessee non-payers of poll-tax and Virginia non-payers of capitation tax. Convicts, criminals, idiots, insane, bribers, and soldiers of the United States Army are commonly disqualified. Duellists are denied voting power in Florida, Michigan, South Carolina, Virginia, and Wisconsin.

Other restrictions and enlargements are quite possible. So far as I could gather the national tendency, I am inclined to think that before long the suffrage will – within, of course, wholesome bounds – be somewhat restricted. There is a sort of warning in the Presidential message of December last, which, if carried into law, may deprive of suffrage many present voters, whose sympathies are manifestly alien to the land of their adoption.

I have alluded to Territories as distinguished from States. A Territory is a State in process of formation. The settlement of the vast area west of the original States, which fringed the Atlantic seaboard, require its being broken into parcels of a size practicable for governing purposes, and necessitates some such embrionic stage. When a Territory has a sufficient population (fixed originally at 5,000), a governor, Secretary, and Judges are provided, and a Legislative Council of its own inhabitants is selected by Congress. The Territory sends to the House of Representatives one delegate, popularly elected, who has all the power of a Congressman, except the power to vote. When the Territory is properly organised, it can, by a convention of its people, become, with the consent of Congress, organised as a State, and be received into the Union. Thus provision is made for receiving, in process of time, into the Union new States, to be composed of the Territories now existing, and of others still to be formed out of the wilderness. A provision is reserved in the Constitution for creating new States from States of unwieldy size; and several of the existing States have thus been formed. In the Act of Congress for the annexation of Texas in 1845, power is reserved of creating out of the existing

Republic of Texas four other States, should both that State itself and the United States, at some future time, mutually desire it.

One cannot help being struck with the practical nature of the Americans. The spirit everywhere manifests itself – sometimes in a form quite inconvenient to those who evoke a hostile feeling. In the reform of abuses we can see its quick and ready working. When I was in Cincinnati two years ago a leading lawyer said to me: 'Something will occur here before long, for the administration of justice is at present a farce. There are at present eight murderers in the gaol waiting trial. They were nearly everyone caught redhanded, but I will venture to say that not one of them will be hanged.' A month later a flagrant judicial outrage was perpetrated. The people suddenly rose and burned down the Courthouse and the gaol; the guilty officials had to fly for their lives. Ever since, I understand, the administration of justice in Cincinnati has been unattended with complaint. Again, at the Presidential election a year ago, frauds were suspected in Cook County, Illinois – the County in which Chicago is situated. It was a gigantic evil to grapple with, but a few leading citizens of different political views got together, and formed, by degrees, a committee of a hundred, which they increased to five hundred, and then to a thousand, and commenced an investigation, which resulted in the punishment of more than a hundred election judges. At the same election, a riot, in New York City, was apprehended, which would have been attended with most disastrous consequences. At the election of 1876, Tilden, the Democratic Candidate, had been 'counted out,' as it is euphemistically called by Hayes, and the New Yorkers, who send to the Electoral College 36 representatives – the largest number of any State in the Union – were determined not to let any fraud be, on this occasion, perpetrated. The result of the elections should have been known on the evening of Tuesday, 4th November. But the returns were not made and the suspicions of intended frauds grew with increasing intensity every hour. By the following Friday political feeling was red-hot. I spent the Friday night amongst the newspaper offices, where reports were coming in every few minutes, and it was everywhere anticipated that if a declaration was not made in the morning there would be fighting in the streets before nightfall.

This strength of feeling will be better understood when we bear in mind that one party advocated Civil Service reform, which President Cleveland is now carrying out, whilst the other took as a watchword 'To the victors the spoils,' which meant the patronage to every Civil Service post in the United States. In Washington City alone there is quite an army of clerks. The Civil Service of the United States embraces over 100,000 persons, and every post might given an opening for a political job.

In social matters, too, action, when taken to mend abuses, is quick; two instances I may give. At my first visit to New York, I was taken by the police over the criminal section of the city. I there saw vice in an open form which amazed me, even when I remembered Paris fifteen years ago; but when I visited New York a year after, there was an almost inconceivable change for the better. Again, a year ago, in Chicago, the manner and quantity of gambling, which was openly allowed, was terrible to think of. The gambling saloons were in leading streets, and were open all night long. I have never seen anything more pitiful than the workmen's gambling saloons, where every vice that cupidity can suggest was given in *duodecimo*. But within a few months a strong movement shook the system to the dust, and the last I heard was that the gamblers were looking for the hulk of a vessel, which they might moor in the lake, and form a saloon outside the city bounds.

In another way the practical spirit was manifested when the time of day was fixed by an arbitrary division of the country into four parallel sections running north and south – Eastern, Central, Mountain, and Western – the time of each division, going westwards, being an exact hour behind the preceding one. This change from solar to standard time was effected silently and in one day, although, perhaps, touching the habits of a larger number of persons than were directly influenced by the adoption of the Gregorian calendar.

It must not be for an instant imagined that because the Americans are practical they are devoid of sentiment; on the contrary, the national sentiment is a strong as that of any other country I know, and I have never met, in my own experience, a want of sentiment in individuals. The national sentiment may well be strong, for it is but twenty years since a war, which was based on a national sentiment, raged through the land. We never knew much of that war – the War of the Union – and now that the graves are hidden with the 'sweet oblivion of flowers,' we can only know or guess what it was from the dry pages of books and statistics of the ruin which it caused.

In that war, which lasted from 1861 to 1865, nearly a million of men – the flower of the people – were slain in actual battle, or died from diseases acquired; 6,000,000 of men passed through the hospitals. The Public Debt, which in 1860 was $64,600,000, swelled between that date and 1867 – when the bills were in – to $2,773,200,000. It has been my good fortune to have met with many men who took part in that terrible war, and their descriptions seemed to open out a whole panorama of thought. In the War of Independence, when England was the foe, the total loss was some 27,000 men; yet at the battle of Chickamauga (which of us remembers or ever knew the name?) the loss on both sides was 33,000 men, at Petersburg it was 38,000, at the Wilderness, 49,000, and at Gettysburg 54,000.

My first personal experience of national sentiment was the first time I crossed the Atlantic. Amongst other games we had on board what they call a 'tug of war,' where equal numbers at opposite ends of a rope try to draw their opponents across a line. We had some twenty on each side, and the opponents were England and America. Well, the first time England won; then we tried again. This time we English were pulled right over the line with a rapidity which we could not understand. On investigation, we found that some seventeen persons, chiefly ladies, had joined our opponents, and were aiding in the game; there they stood, with panting bosoms and flashing eyes. I could hardly understand their ardour then. I understood it better later on: when, everywhere in the Northern States – in New England, by the southern shores of the chain of lakes, and in the cities of the Western prairies – I saw the monuments of the dead heroes of that War of the Union; when, on the Southern border, in the track of the great battles, I saw everywhere the new homesteads arisen on the ruins of the old; and when I stood on Arlington heights, and looked over the broad waters of the Potomac at the splendour of the Federal City of Washington that lay beyond, whilst I wandered in that Campo Santo of the nation's heroes amongst the stretching miles of graves.

In other ways, too, there are evidences of national sentiment. I remember how I was struck when, on Washington's birthday, I came through Boston Common and saw the equestrian statue of the nation's hero rising grimly from the waste of snow, his neck circled with a wreath of summer flowers. Again, with the touching inscription on the base of the statue to Admiral Farragut, in New York, which tells that the statue was erected 'that those who shall come after him and who shall owe him so much, shall see him as he was ever seen by friend and foe.' Again, when, as a sort of peaceoffering and emblem of goodwill to the Southern States, Pennsylvania sent to the Exhibition at New Orleans the 'Liberty Bell,' as it is called, the bell of the old Independence Hall of Philadelphia, where the Declaration was signed. It went through the country, heralded everywhere with joy, brought on its way to the sound of music, and gay with ribbons and flowers.

The correlative of sentiment, humour, is in nowise wanting. There is everywhere, latent or apparent, a strong sense of humour. It is mainly of a dry kind. In Chicago I saw a notice on the side of a house where there was an office in the basement, whose entrance was protected by a balustrade:–

'WANTED.
'A LOAFER TO SIT ON THIS RAIL.'

In Fourth Avenue, New York, there is an inscription beside the cigar lighter in a tobacconist's shop:–

'Take care you light it well; it will save trouble to the Recording Angel.'

The spirit of content may be illustrated by the piety of a negro preacher, whose sustenance was entirely reliant on the offertory of his little congregation – the usual method in the coloured churches. The flock did not seem to at all respond to the appeal. The pastor's hat, which served as poor plate, was passed from one to another, but without result. The minister saw that his luxuries for the following week would be *nil*; then that his comforts must be abandoned; and, finally, that the very necessaries of life were not forthcoming. The hat was brought to him. He took it by the middle of the crown and held it up and shook it – but nothing came forth. He turned up his eyes and said resignedly:–

'Bress de Lord! Bress de good Lord dat I got back my hat!'

I heard of a Western man who, having come to New York, determined to try that greatest of American luxuries, the canvas-back duck. He went to Delmonico's, the great restaurant in Fifth Avenue, and ordered one. Now, the canvas-back duck is a bird of very considerable *embonpoint*, and has in itself resources in the way of gravy which would have satisfied even the boarders of Mrs. Todgers. The bird is generally lightly cooked. The saying is, that you must carry it through a moderately warm kitchen. When the bird was cut it was brought to the customer, swimming in red gravy. He looked at it critically.

'Yes,' he said, 'yes, that will do very nicely. Just will you, like a good fellow, take it away and kill it.'

One great trait of character is observable – that a joke is taken in good part. Of course, there are nasty people all the world over, who can neither give nor take becomingly; but, in my own experience, I found universally a tolerant good humour and a hearty appreciation of anything which was worthy. As I went through America with my friend, Henry Irving, I had a good opportunity of observing the critical faculty of the people and I found them everywhere exceedingly fair and unprejudiced, with a remarkable receptivity, and 'no allowance' – as the sailors say – in their expression of approval when pleased. I honestly believe that no artist could ask a fairer or better audience, or one before whom he would be content to make his best effort, than is to be found anywhere between Maine and California. Mr. Irving expressed strongly his views on this subject in an article in the *Fortnightly Review*. Miss Ellen Terry must, I fancy, be in doubt as to whether she conquered the country or was conquered by the hospitality and enthusiasm of its people.

One instance of conquering I must mention, for it touches the fame of a dear friend. It was when Henry Irving gave an address on the 'Art of Acting' in Harvard University. It was the first time in the two centuries and a-half of its history that such an honour had been paid in the University to an actor, and it meant a sweeping away of prejudice, which only knowledge of an old Puritan community can make understood.

I remember well how proud we, friends and Englishmen, were as we saw before the whole strength and intellect of the University the actor's distinguished face, rising above a sea of heads, whilst in the eloquent inscription* behind was traced the story of Englishmen who, flying from intolerance, had found a home in the leafy wilderness.

Hic in silvestribus
et incultis locis
Angli domo profugi
Anno post Christum Natum MDCXXXVI.
Post Coloniam hue deductam VI.
Sapientiam rati ante omnia colendam
Scholam publice condiderunt
Conditam Christo et Ecclesiae dicaverunt
Quae aucta Johannis Harvard munificentia
a litterarum fautoribus cum nostratibus tum externis
identidem adjuta
Alumnorum denique fidei commissa
ab exiguis perducta initiis ad majora rerum incrementa
praesidum sociorum inspectorum sentaus academici
consiliis et prudentia et cura
optimas artes virtutes publicas privatas
coluit colit
'Qui antem docti fuerint fulgebunt quasi splendor firmamente
et qui ad justitiam erudiunt multos
quasi stellae in perpetuas aetermitates.'

Truly the tide of prejudice of the centuries had rolled back, and the Old World and the New, each working out its destiny, had met on common ground, and from every side the old intolerance was a thing of the past.

There is no doubt whatever that there is throughout America a widespread tolerance. Surely it is a noble substratum on which to build the temple of a nation's greatness. Its spirit has become written law in nearly all the State Constitutions. That the Nation has not risen from or sunk to indifference in religious matters – wherein is the gauge of toleration – is shown in the fact that in the States, which have in their Bill of Rights proclaimed freedom of worship, provision is made by purely voluntary effort for the accommodation of the people. Thus in Vermont and Ohio – both of which proclaim religion of all kinds free – the number of seats provided in the various places of worship is equal to the number of the entire population over ten years of age. We do not, I understand, nearly arrive at a similar result in the United Kingdom, in England, or even in London.

My feeling of the sentiment, and my experience of the working of the institutions of the United States, satisfies me that in future development, of country, or of race, or of policies which are to sway the world, we need never fear the developments of Popular Government. I mention this, not in any party spirit, but because my attention was called to it by what seems to me the imperfect conclusions of Sir Henry Maine, based on an examination of the working of the American Constitution.

Lastly, I took away with me from the shores of America a feeling of love and gratitude towards its people, and one of joy that England's first-born child has arrived at so noble a stature.

We have not, all the world through, so strong an ally, so close a friend. America has got over her childhood. The day of petty jealousy has gone by. Columbia is strong enough in her knowledge of her own power and beauty to sail, unruffled and unawed, into the salon of old Time amidst the queens of the world. There is every reason we can think of why the English on both sides of the Atlantic should hold together as one. Our history is their history – our fame is their pride – their progress is our glory. They are bound to us, and we to them, by every tie of love and sympathy; on our side, by the bright hopes of parents who send their children to seek fortune in the Sunset Land; on theirs, by the old remembrances of home and common kin, and by the memories of their buried dead. We are bound each to each by the instinct of a common race, which makes brotherhood and the love of brothers a natural law; a law which existed at the first, and which, after the lapse of a century, still exists – whose tenets were never broken, even by the shocks of war, and whose keen perception was never dimmed in the wilderness of stormy sea between.

28 December 1885
London Institution

Trinity Address

The Necessity for Political Honesty

The Auditor, Mr. Abraham Stoker, A.B., delivered the opening Address: After which it was proposed by the Right Hon. John Thomas Ball, Q.C., LL.D., M.P.; seconded by Rev. George A. Chadwick, and resolved:– 'That the thanks of the Society be given to the Auditor for his Address.' It was proposed by Dr. Shaw, F.T.C.D., seconded by Mr. Gerald Fitzgibbon, Q.C., and resolved:– 'That the Auditor's Address be printed at the expense of the Society.' The President then awarded the Society's Prizes as follows:–

Oratory:
Gold Medal – Miles V. Kehoo, A.B.
Silver Medal – H. Tydd Lane, A.B., *Rec. Sec.*
Certificates – R. Valentine Fitzgerald, A.B. Charles M. Arundell, Charles L. Matheson, *Cor. Sec.* Rev. J. M'Millan. A.B., A. Stoker, A.B., *Auditor*, W. O'Shaughnessy, A.B., W. T. King.
History:
Gold Medal – Peter C Farrell, A.B.
Composition:
President's Gold Medal – Charles M Arundell
Society's Silver Medal – W. O'Shaughnessy, A.B.,

The Prize of Ten Guineas offered by Mr. Edward Gibson, Q.C., Ex-Auditor, Hon. Mem., for the best Essay on University Education in Ireland, was awarded to Albert W. Quill, A.B., Ex-Auditor.

Mr President and Gentlemen,

Standing as I do upon this platform, as the representative of the Historical Society, I dare not speak one word to-night which from my heart and soul I do not believe to be true. The sense of responsibility is so heavy on me that I could not, even if I would, but be deeply moved. For between the Past and the Future we now stand; the men of a hundred years are grouped behind us – the dead and the living linked together in our minds by our old traditions, and I trust that before us lies the grander assemblage of more centuries than one. A successor to those who have passed and who guard by their memories that which in their lives they loved and worked for, I cannot feel other than unworthy to claim, even for a moment, a kinship with them. But when I think of the Future, and that in this Hall to-night are many men on whom an honest word spoken from the heart, may have some effect; for good, I feel awed by the tremendous responsibility of my position.

In such a difficulty I have no help from aught save perfect simplicity, no resource but truth; and so I will ask you to let the honesty of my purpose atone for the deficiencies of my powers. I have chosen, as the theme of my address, the NECESSITY FOR POLITICAL HONESTY, because such seems to me to be the grandest subject that the whole world of thought affords to young men. Whatever we may think or say, Gentlemen, we are beginning our public life in taking part in the working of this old Society; and at the threshold of our lives there is, surely, no subject which touches us so deeply as that which contains the germs of our future. Success or failure awaits us according to how we work, and it is vitally important that we should begin properly, that we may not be doomed to failure at the very start. I hold that the same rules of right and wrong, which are our springs of personal action, should be through life our guides in state matters, and that the only policy whose effects will for ever influence the world for good, is that which is but the enlargement and perfection of our personal truth and justice. I will only speak out my own convictions on the matter, for the limit of time forbids me to attempt proofs of what I assert. I will simply speak as a young man to young men, for I feel that in so doing I shall best perform my duty; and so, show my gratitude to those who have placed me here: and if I can succeed in awaking a high thought in one young soul, I shall not have spoken in vain.

But before attempting to speak at all of politics, it may be advisable to consider briefly the position which the Historical Society at present occupies in the University, in order that we may see why the Necessity for Political Honesty is a subject of peculiar importance to us. Here, however, I must preface the inquiry by stating clearly and positively that I do not advocate any change whatever, in either the constitution or the working of the Society, for no reform is needed. And you are not for an instant to imagine that in speaking of the Historical Society as the political training school of the University, I hold that it does, or that it ought to teach the maxims of any, or all, political parties; but that I consider it to be a school in which men are trained to be politicians. I merely wish that we should clearly understand the position which we occupy, and how politics come to be a legitimate topic of interest with us. Our opportunity for self-culture depends in a great measure on the knowledge which we have of our own powers, so that we may know how best to exercise them, and consequently it is a matter of primary importance with us that we take a correct estimate of ourselves.

There are, doubtless, many persons who think that the Historical Society is in exactly the same state now as it was at its foundation in 1770, or at least at its revival in 1843; but to such persons I will endeavour to show that not only has its purpose by degrees vastly changed, but that its prosperity has depended and still depends on this very change.

To say that the Historical Society should always remain the same and yet retain its efficiency, would be to assert that whilst all the rest of the world sweeps onward on the wings of progress, it alone stands still. But the contrary is the case. It bases its claim to support, not on the quicksand of popular favour, but on the rock of usefulness. It cannot live tolerated, and whilst it cherishes as its noblest heirlooms its old traditions, it does not content itself with their mere possession; it lives not in the past alone, but makes its past in each generation. It is no ornamental appanage to the College, but is its supplementary school, and it must always keep its relative position with it in its progress if it is to live and flourish. The cause of the change is to be found in the growing usefulness of the College. As the curriculum of the University widened to suit the demands made for higher education, the College absorbed much of the special teaching function of the Society, and the gap thus made had to be filled up. Thus the change was effected perforce, and as occasion demanded what had become effete was cleared away before the march of necessity. The object of the Historical Society at its foundation, and again at its revival, was the cultivation of history, oratory, and literature – subjects at even the later date sadly neglected in the University. Of late years, however, the study of literature and history has made rapid advances, and these subjects are now taught in the schools. A collegiate society can never successfully attempt to rival the professional teaching, and so when the importance of these studies began to be recognised, the Society was obliged to relinquish their special cultivation.

Nothing seemed to remain now as a speciality, except oratory. But oratory is not in itself a sufficient object for a body like ours. It is an art as well as a science – it needs practice as well as theory; and the aspiring speaker must have some materials with which to work. We can no more practice oratory, as an art by itself, than we can chisel a statue from the air, or work an engine without fuel. Not the mere articulation of syllables, but the expression of ideas makes an orator, and, without ideas to express, his words are as

– a tale
'Told by an idiot, full of sound and fury,
Signifying nothing.'

And this is more especially true in our own age, in which oratory is the earnest exposition of fact, and where the Registrar-General is the armourer of the orator.

Accordingly some study whose expression would cultivate the powers of speaking became a necessity, and with us, that subject arose from the slow-grown want in the University of a political training school. As the old purely literary and historical questions of debate began to fall into disuse, their place was supplied by questions which bore more or less on the great problems of the day – not those of party significance, but those important to the nation at large; and the number of these practical questions has of late years been steadily on the increase. The change has been slow and silent, but not the less powerful on that account, for changes from within are all-powerful; and it has been a good one, for it followed slowly the progress of the age, gaining a little with each collegiate generation. It did not arise from the love of change, but from the necessity for it: and now at last, this necessity, which is the parent of all just reform, has given us a society which supplements the teaching of the University; where questions of general politics may be discussed without acrimony; and which teaches that style of speaking which suits the requirements of the age.

Such is the present position of our Society, and such is the gradual change, which is just the manifestation of Progress amongst us. In these days of politics when every man, young and old, is acquainted in some degree with the condition of state affairs, and when criticism has become a science, it would be absolutely impossible to prevent discussion. Even if the subjects for debate were to be limited to the merest dry-as-dust questions of history, our members could and would find a way of expressing their opinions as to the things around them. This is a practical age as to working; and when men learn that, to the quality of the arms which they wield, and to the experience which they have of their use, they must look for success, they will not be content to spend all their youth in practising with toy swords and dummy guns, but must have the real weapons with which to exercise. If they cannot get what they want here they will elsewhere; and in such case the value of our old traditions will be lost to them, for they will start in life without that sense of responsibility of trust handed down to them, which tends to keep men honest and true. But long ago the governing body of the College, seeing that the discussion of questions of general politics could not with benefit be repressed, allowed a silent and gradual change to take place; and finding that increased opportunity brought with it increased respect for institutions and higher purpose, and withal a greater breadth of view, they still allowed the change to go on, and acknowledged by their toleration the progress of the Society, as well as its importance.

And wisely they countenanced the change, and allowed the Society to perform its functions unfettered; for like all other educational bodies it must have freedom, or at least a certain latitude, or its efforts can be but of little real use. The function of the Historical Society clashes in no wise with that of the College. It represents self-culture, whereas the latter exemplifies instruction. The teaching body of a college or university cannot instruct in every branch of human wisdom; it must leave much to self-culture, and the line at which it should stop should be that of established fact. It may teach abstractions which are recognized as truths by the world at large, but it cannot safely indulge in the hazardous exploits of experimentalism. Here it is that the value of our Society as a supplemental school is most clearly shown. Whilst performing its primary function of teaching oratory, it gives the student his first lesson in politics, by teaching him to apply to the circumstances which surround him, the truths garnered from history, and the experience of men and ages – to forestall by his reason the results of practice; and to do this at a time when he is still unprejudiced by the issues which he investigates and able to judge impartially. In the great world of politics the value of discussion is to find from the reason and acuteness of many trained minds, the result of certain combinations, which result should agree with the issue of trial; and in this respect our Society is the House of Parliament in miniature. But its function is not merely to afford an opportunity for self-culture – it encourages study and deliberation. By directing the force of our united wills to one common object, we form a public opinion of our own which turns the thoughts of beginners into the proper channel, and by giving a young man an opportunity of expressing his opinions on the questions which most interest him, we encourage him to study each of those questions in all its bearings. Having so examined it he is apt to take a more correct view of it than if he had merely adopted a perhaps one-sided opinion of some friend, or formed his judgment upon a few isolated facts remembered from casual study. Instead then of being confused by the vast array of facts and theories which buzz around his ears from the great organs of public expression, he finds his attention called to the various questions in detail; and as each is thoroughly weighed and sifted, according to his powers, it takes its place in the true experience of the student, and becomes part of his knowledge, whilst it has played its temporary part in the development of his understanding. By letting him see that his opinions, when formed by himself, will be justly and fearlessly criticised by others, he is taught to be careful, and by the union of opportunity and criticism, he learns to study, to think, to be generous, and to be just. There is no young man, such as we have amongst us, but would wish to have the approval of his fellows; and when in our debates men find that bigotry and prejudice and cynicism are looked on as worse faults than ignorance, they soon learn to be liberal in their views, and tolerant of the opinions of others. Even in the last few years, when the whole country was agitated with the renewal of old strife and old disaffection, and when great reforms, religious and territorial, were carried out, their effects were debated without a shadow of ill-will, here, amongst a body of men whose future they vitally influenced.

Such opportunities the Historical Society presents to students; but to grasp them, it is necessary to cast off all unworthy prejudice, and to let the better part of nature have free play. Moral and intellectual benefits are, like the San Graal, only to be found by those who have cast off, so far as they can, the dross of mortality. The baser parts of us, and those which are most apt to manifest themselves – cynicism and sophistry – are not attributes of youth; they are the world's lessons taught to the old by years of disappointment, but to youth they are untrue. Besides let no man think that cynicism is the high road to success. The leaders of the world are not cynics, but enthusiasts, and to their honesty and purpose is progress due. The true motive power of life is enthusiasm, and to the young it is natural. But without honesty this glorious gift of youth – its strength, its hope, its soul, is dead; for who is there that can feel one spark of passion in a cause when his heart is not his guide? And doing right with us is no mere matter of pleasure, but one of duty; we have been given ten talents to use, and the responsibility of the trust keeps pace with the hope of the reward.

We young men should not be players when we ought to work; and we should, so far as we are able, look at all questions, not as boys, but as men. Tyros are we now, it is true, but in time we shall be veterans, for the boyhood of one age is the strong manhood of the next. We are indulging in no day-dreams when we try to the best of our ability to puzzle out the truth amongst us from many conflicting opinions. But if we wish to find the truth, we must be absolutely just; and the practice of justice is the beginning of political honesty. 'As the twig is bent, the tree inclines' and as we are straight or warped now, so shall we continue till the end. In taking part in the debates of this society – for mere listening is of little use – we enter that road which leads to the highest honours of the state. Men who have a right to make us value their words – men whom we in this society reverence as the lights and adornments of their age, have over and over again told us that in this very hall was the beginning of their success; that here the emulation and the honest criticism of their equals taught them generosity, justice, and truth. What they have achieved is open to us all; but if like them we wish to succeed, we must do as they did – work hard and strive to avoid the taints of prejudice. It would be folly to say that we must all succeed, or that we should all be worthy of like success; it would be untrue to say that many of us hope for such honour in our wildest dreams, but to those who are patient and who work, the honour, if they are worthy of it, will come in time.

As to the means by which we may best train ourselves, I conceive that each man should give, so far as possible, the reins to his own genius. Our rules of order are sufficiently strict to make good taste a necessary observance in the debates; and the grand rule of free action *Laissez faire* should allow each man to choose or mould his own construction of argument, and his manner of expressing it. But let us be true, I say again and again, or we are nothing. We *never* can atone by after effort or by education and experience for the falsehood of youth. Our ignorance is more boundless than our knowledge can ever be; and it is only by using properly the little which we do know – by speaking out our thoughts honestly, without fear, and without being prejudiced in favour of our expressed views by the mere expression of them, that we can really educate ourselves. We may seem to learn, but in reality it is only the negative becoming positive – the void of our ignorance being filled up with untruth. And as men beginning our political career, we should have ever before us the noblest object for which man can work – the advancement of truth, and as its perfection that truth which in public affairs is as widely different from partizanship, and class feeling and self interest, as it is from dishonesty and selfishness in private matters. As truth broadens out from individuals to nations, so should we have in view its teaching, not only to persons, but to the world at large. And to raise the nation or the individual ever so little, we must hope and work for much, and have a high ideal standard towards the realization of which all our efforts may tend. We here, most of all must join in hoping for one common end, and have it ever before us, our pillar of cloud by day and of flame by night to lead us to the Canaan of our hopes. Such a guide is necessary to us, for without it we can have no settled purpose; and such guide is the same to us now, and for all our lives. In the rush and hurry of the world in which we live, where conflicting interests rise like barriers to our advancement whithersoever we turn – in the doubt and perplexity that everywhere enshroud us, there is only one true policy, and that is to struggle for what we believe to be the right, through storm and trial, through sunshine and tears, no matter what difficulties we have to encounter – no matter what may be the consequence to ourselves. Society, as it exists amongst us, both political and social, is rapidly becoming effete; and the only hope which remains for its regeneration is that we may yet be able to carry into it some of that personal purity which still exists with individuals. So many influences work for the corruption of mankind that the amelioration of society cannot be unconsciously effected, and we who propound the truth must also teach it by example. Should we then be backward in affording our aid when the future rests with us?

In advocating the cause of political honesty I fear that I have a great difficulty to encounter, for there are many who doubtless think indignantly that my advocacy imputes sinister motives to them, and others who pityingly imagine that to expect political purity is to dream a foolish dream. To the former of these I would say that the present honesty existing in political affairs is not enough. The politicians of the day have been reared in a school in which the notions of right and wrong in state affairs were not at all those in personal affairs. We are, I hope, honest individuals, but we have not yet been tried as honest politicians; and when we see many men like ourselves gradually giving way to the great force of self-interest brought to bear on them from the very fact of their entrance into public life, we may well fear for our own future, and take care, so far as we can, that our training will enable us to resist these temptations when they come. To those who admit the truth of the theory of perfect honesty in politics, but are disbelievers in the possibility of its practice, I would say that that seeming impossibility which is their stumbling-block is one of the old errors which must pass away.

In this age in which cynicism is too often considered ability, and in which the worker and his critics are creatures of different worlds, the advocacy of an ideal honesty may seem as wild as the dreams of Don Quixote; and this one idea only will I therefore venture to put forward, and urge with what force I can – that we should have a theory in which we have perfect belief, and which we may ceaselessly endeavour to carry into practice. We are here now not as practical politicians, but as theorists; and we are learning the principles which will guide and mould our future deeds. Our time of action will come soon enough, and in trial and temptation, when the lessons which we have here learned have borne us in safety through the flame, we will be grateful for the theoretic teaching which brought us forth unscathed. I appeal to men behind me – men with the experience – the personal experience of half a century in the world of facts, to tell you that unless theory is sound practice is at best a chance. It may be that affairs are regulated for a time by it, and that the issue seems good till tested: but in the end, when the time of trial comes, he who trusts in practice without theory finds out too late that in scorning the belief in a possible perfection, he has fallen into the error of a blind credulity in what is weak.

On three great grounds – Moral, Utilitarian, and Patriotic – we should have as our object of ambition Political Honesty – the testing as just or unjust in itself, as well as taken in connection of the great scheme of which it is a part, every proposed measure which is to affect the community.

The first ground – Morality – I put forward, lest any one should think that we wish to be honest, because, in the words of the proverb, 'honesty is the best policy.' The religion which we all receive in common, howsoever we may differ in its forms, teaches is that whatever the consequences may be, we should act according to our belief. We hold this rule as the guiding principle of our private lives, and the recognition of it in public matters is only carrying it out in its perfection. We should trust our consciences rather than our heads, for false education and perverted opportunities may have weakened our power of reason; but the conscience is the diviner part of man – it may become as dormant, but it never can be perverted or warped.

But there is no necessity for being guided blindly by the conscience, since a little reflection will satisfy our reason, and show us that in politics honesty is the most correct practical rule. Both in detail for the solution of the state problems with which we have at present to grapple, and in the abstract as a guiding principle, Political Honesty is the high road to the nation's safety and greatness.

Just consider for a moment the position in which we stand, and you will see the great necessity for political purity, both for our protection and our progress. There is war without and war within. The force of nationalities is manifesting itself, and in the settling down of races are such mighty upheavals that our little country is in danger of being crushed. States which we used to consider as collectively not our equals in force are becoming so great, that unless our growth keeps pace with theirs, we must eventually be stifled. We cannot increase in territory, we cannot increase much more in numbers; but in liberality and honesty there are no bounds to progress; and when we have ceased to be the mart of the world, we may become the arbiter of its destinies and its temple of justice. All around us ancient forms are being renewed, and new ones cropping up. The spirits of Caesar and Brutus rise from the slumber of eighteen centuries, and United Germany marches us on the one hand, and Republican France on the other. The Slavonic nations awake from their long lethargy, and Russia with her millions threatens the future peace of Europe, and stretches already a greedy arm towards British India. Another Reformation, not by theologians, but by politicians, is at hand, and the bells are being founded that axe to ring the death-knell of the union of Church and State throughout the world. Across the Atlantic, not now an illimitable waste but a strait crossed by a bridge of boats, the great Republic, a century old, is growing so vast that the merits and demerits of ideal democracy may ere long be tested.

And even here, this vast nation splitting up into factions, whose collision would effect materially the progress of our affairs. At home the strife of labour and capital, so ruinous to a commercial country, is carried on with increasing bitterness, and a actual want stares many of our people in the face. The influence of individuals for good or ill is struggling for supremacy, with the force of many, united, to gain one temporary advantage; and the educated *one* contends against the ignorant, *en masse*. Add to these difficulties the hollowness and artificialness of society within, and its wastefulness and extravagance without, and you will see in what a plight we really are. Who is to see the end of all these things; what statesman were he even gifted with tenfold force of intellect can see even the probable solution of the difficulty? So interwoven are the myriad warps and wefts in the giant web of the world that on attempting investigation we have to fall back amazed and abashed. Try to follow even one thread, and after a moment your intellect will fail, and your eyes grow dim from the intensity of your fruitless gaze; but to consider the whole fabric were indeed a task. Every thing is so gigantic now-a-days that no man should hope to match his puny intellect against the vast combinations of forces which surround him. And yet we see statesmen trying to subordinate every circumstance to their own schemes, and to form a maze of political combinations, of which they alone may hold the clue. And further, we see men who are blind enough and credulous enough to support them in all their schemes – who fulfil their behests by weight of numbers, and make laws and carry reforms, knowing often that the things which they do or sanction are wrong in themselves. They put the faith that should only be given to God in the intellects of men, and support false measures under the flimsy pretext that, although they are wrong in themselves, the scheme of which they are a necessary part is, in the main, right. Such men are fools where they are not corrupt, for they should know that every deed, every law which is intended for the ultimate benefit of the nation should be based on principle, and a principle admits of no compromise. Legislation in which the smallest flaw is discernible is bad – if put to the severest test, that flaw, though seeming trivial, will cause its ruin. For the statesman and the philosopher all times and all ages blend into one vast cycle; and the merits of every change will be tested by the great and not the little period; nations as mighty as we have ever been have fallen, and we can, after the lapse of centuries, trace out the causes of their fall, and see what mighty disasters rose from beginnings so small as to be lost in the lapse of time. Why then will we permit deeds to be done and laws made which are manifestly imperfect? Why will we allow the reins of State to be held often by men whose acts and omissions show them to be either weak or insincere? Why will we support such men and give all the assistance in our power to their schemes? Some of these statesmen – men of unblemished reputation in their private lives – men whom a vast body of the population regard with a feeling almost of veneration, seem to believe that a nation can beneficially be governed by a system of political sleight-of-hand; they appear to consider that Janus is the statesman's exemplar, and that his endeavour should be to deceive all parties with whom he comes in contact. Instead of grappling with questions of vital importance, whose delay hour by hour is a drag upon the nation in her race with the nations of the world, they seek shelter in avoidance, and seem to think that because they shut their eyes to an evil it therefore ceases to exist.

Compare with these statesmen the grand example before the eyes of the poet who wrote of the great Irishman – the greatest general that the world e'er saw –

'The world's victor's victor,

Who never sold the truth to serve the hour,

Or paltered with Eternal God for power.'

Think which is, for us, the grander ideal, and judge for yourselves if a noble end is to be attained by crooked means.

Surely, it is a noble scheme to carry into the affairs of the nation, where every act done means happiness or misery – peace or strife – content or vexation to millions, the truth and honour which regulate our private lives. In so much as the nation is greater than the individual, who is but an integral part of it, is the need in its government for the same regulating principle of truth but a more rigid exactness in its application. In our private lives we see how every little breach of truth is multiplied in its after effects – how great then must be the evil resulting from untruth in the state? In our private lives our only safeguard is in our habitual practice of truth, for in every new danger it dictates our mode of action before reason and experience would have time to advise. And in state affairs the habit of just dealing is, if possible, more necessary, for no man can, by his own wisdom, or his own powers and experience, no matter how great, be prepared against every contingency that may happen. Napoleon tried it – and failed; and when his splendid intellect was unequal to the strain, it would be presumptuous folly for lesser minds to attempt the task. But haply temptations like his cannot again occur. The influence of individuals in so unqualified a manner, as it often existed, has declined; the age of diplomacy has passed and that of arbitration, for individuals, bodies, and nations, is at hand. The duel has given place to the civil action, the strike has been superseded by the conference of masters and men, and the war has been avoided by the convention. Never again, whilst science and education remain to us can any man hope to sway, by his own capricious behaviour the destinies of the world, or to trap nations into compromising situations by the exercise of cunning. He may wield the sceptre by the force of great principles which he trusts in and develops, but he cannot rule in security by caprice. It is a war of Titans, not men – a war of principles which will convulse the future – and what principle is so potent, so everlasting, in its force as truth? If we act steadfastly up to our own belief we must eventually be right. It is possible that from want of experience we may for a time go astray, but we shall by degrees find out our errors and correct them; for increase of education will show us what is best. Our principle should be, not to follow any one scheme of policy which men have framed, but to do always what we believe is right, even if the honest change of our conduct in particular affairs should give our enemies an opportunity to call us fickle. We are not cowards that we should fear being called renegades for changing our views, when we feel that in doing so we are right. To the just there is no earthly praise so sweet as the approval of their own souls; and, strong in our consciousness of truth, we can afford to despise our calumniators. We are not traitors to a cause because we are ingenuous to ourselves and honest to the world at large. That cause has little basis in truth, and little chance of ultimate success, which seeks to bind men to it by self-interest or fear, and the sooner it is abandoned the better; but a really noble cause rests on its own merits and seeks not to enforce allegiance from any man; and such a cause will eventually prosper. In spite of all opposition the right must succeed. The end may be delayed – we may wait for long through the darkness, but the dawn will surely come.

But not alone directly is honesty beneficial – the moral force of consistent truth is enormous. The old English romancers had a noble ideal in view when they made Galahad, the type of purity, pass unscathed through all dangers, and come out victorious from every fray. If we fight our battle under the oriflamme of truth, we must be victorious also. By a belief in our cause we gain half the battle, for we do not dread defeat – we may fall, but we fall with a glorious hope. Self-belief and self-reliance can only spring from habitual faith, and the issue is the same for a nation as well as an individual, for a nation is the agglomerate of all its individuals. It was no mere hope springing from despair which induced the starving garrison of Lucknow to expect the arrival of succour – it was the belief in British valour which had been tested for a thousand years – the belief in the tried courage and devotedness of their fellow-countrymen, which never yet had failed. In habit do we ever find our unconscious safeguard: and in the habit of honesty shall we find our strength and our safety combined. Belief in our cause, and therefore in ourselves, has ever been the parent of real bravery. It has borne those who felt it through trial and danger, and hardship and pain; and to us, whether we war with men or things – against arms or temptations, or social faults, it will ever bring equal strength. It nerved the arms of our bowmen at Crecy and Poitiers and Agincourt: it withstood the shock of Rupert's cavalry at Naseby; it bore up our soldiery through the deadly hailstorm on the slopes of Waterloo: it met the force of Russia amid surprise and danger through the mists at Inkerman: it swept with the Six Hundred in their death-ride at Balaklava: it took Howard through the vile prisons of Europe: it made Chatham and Wilberforce, and Grattan, speak words of flame: it cheered Galileo in his dungeon, and Bernard Palissy beside his furnace, and Jenner and Simpson in their long weary hours of trial: it bore the brave spirits of the martyrs of all time through the torments of rack and flame. Every great good that mankind has won through suffering attests its power. In senate and camp – in storm and sunshine – in peace and war – in doubt, and danger, and distress, it never yet failed to make men fight bravely, or bear no less bravely the ills of fortune for a noble cause; and in the dungeon, on the rack on the scaffold and at the stake, its wondrous power has been thundered forth to echo through the ages by the passing spirits of the great. It is our strength in the present, and our hope for the future. Let it not pass from us by the slow decay of indifference or the rapid blight of opposition. If it is not ever before our minds we are apt to forget it, and when we do, we walk thenceforward blindly on the road that leads not to the glorious temple of the Just. Oh! let us trust our cause – let the spread of truth and honesty, as well in politics as in private affairs – as well in the senate as at the hearth – be our sole aim. Our hearts will tell us that it is a noble one. Let these glorious principles grow part of our personal honour, if they are not so already, and time will show those of us who live to see the result, that their culture is the true road to greatness, and the secret of the nation's weal.

Truth and justice go hand in hand, and their might is beginning to assert itself. Of late years internationalism has become a great idea in the minds of men, and one which will sway the destinies of the future. What is this internationalism but the dawning of truth – the broadening out of justice from the nations to the world at large – the casting off of the petty chains of local prejudice, and of that quasi-nationality which is the very apotheosis of parochialism – those petty chains which are more cramping than would be the vastest cables that the might of science could forge, for they bind the soul? When will men learn that patriotism is not merely to sneer at and be jealous of surrounding nations, nor to gather all the love and affection with which God has dowered the heart of man into one little spot till it becomes a garden, whilst all the rest of the world remains, for them, a waste? The true patriot is he who wishes his own country to lead the van of thought and action by a good example, and not he who would make all the earth subservient in everything to his own land.

But the old errors are beginning to pass away,
'And slow and sure comes up the golden year.'
Men are finding out that what is best for the world is best for the nation, and that the consolidation of all countries into one common league for good is the true means of peace. Since my immediate predecessor stood on this platform a great step has been taken, which, although springing from what was at best an error, is the beginning of the end of war.

And with the dawn of internationalism and arbitration has come a wider spirit of charity, and a nobler sense of the duties of humanity. Witness it Chicago, when the electric wires flashed over the Rocky Mountains, and under the Atlantic, messages of hope and succour, till the smouldering city on the banks of Michigan became the very ganglion of Christian charity. Witness it Woerth and Forbach, and Weissenbourg and Sedan, when the Red Cross of the Geneva Convention bore the ambulance unscathed from hostile camp to camp. Aye, Gentlemen, every human virtue follows in the wake of truth, and the forerunner of the Millennium is the broadening view of nations.

Internationalism, in its true sense, is but the nationalism of humanity, and opens up a wide prospect of hope. It has a grandeur, indeed, for the youth of our age who start in life dowered with all the qualities which made their fathers great, rich in the wealth of ages – the knowledge wrung from the trials and the troubles of the past, and strong in the belief that the future, with its Jasper City almost in view, holds forth a more glorious promise than the past has ever known. Before their ken the boundaries of nations fade away as if writ on water, their footsteps are never cramped by earth or ocean, and on the wings of truth their souls can range abroad through the world – this world of ours, which might be so glorious, if those who knew the truth would but make it their rule of action. Oh, let us hold this view – let us strive heart and soul for the realization of this grand ideal – and the cold heartless money-grubbers who call themselves the world may sneer at us at will as dreamers. We can afford – not to laugh, for our thoughts must be ever tinged with pity as we reflect on what they lose – but to dream on, unshaken, till our dreams awake the world.

But let no man think that he will love his own land less because he also loves his kind, and the peace and justice, whose realization is the grandest dream of the poet and the philosopher.

'True love in this differs from gold and clay, –
That to divide is not to take away.'

And the more we really care for our own country the dearer to us will be the whole world. And if ever the time should come when Britain's war-cry must be pealed once more, we shall not fail in action, because we have not been prone to strife, nor shall the wish for peace be found to have enervated the hearts of our people. The aim of the rifle-men need not be less deadly than it has been, nor the bayonet points be wavering, nor the serried ranks be broken, because the country has been just. We may have little fear that our soldiers will forget the lessons of their sires, or that they will be craven in battle, because they have been faithful in peace. We shall see that at need the ploughshare can spring again into the sword, and that the people will gather to the battle from desk and counter and work-shop, and fight – not as fanatics or mercenaries, but as true men warring for a cause.

But there is still another reason why we should regard the purity and honesty of our political views as of paramount importance. The voice of patriotism should be heard in our councils as well as that of utility; and there is a cogent reason why we here in the Historical Society in especial should hearken to it – one which involves our love for our country and belief in the future of our race. We are at the heart of the University which is the intellectual centre of Ireland. The College teaches, and we, in our time of maturity, shall teach, not the people directly, but the teachers of the people. Be our professions the Church, the Senate, the Bar, the Platform, or the Press; we may each of us become leaders of opinion. In what ratio then will our honesty or dishonesty – our good lesson or bad, be multiplied when it reaches the masses in another generation? And what may even now be multiplied a thousand-fold will be increased a million-fold when the people – the great mass of the hewers of wood and drawers of water – have learned the lesson, and have become in turn the fountain of political truth. The Celtic race is waking up from its long lethargy, and another half century will see a wondrous change in the position which it occupies amongst the races of the world. Just conceive what the teaching of a principle may be by the Irish in America alone. There the development of the race is a patent fact. Far and wide from Atlantic to Pacific, in cities and cultivated lands, and in the great wilds, the Ireland of half a century back is renewing its youth, and in vast numbers swelling the population of the Western Republic. Those who have travelled through the land, say that these very people – aye, even in the second and third generation – even those to whom Ireland is as was Eden to the children of Seth, still refer to it as *home*. Think for a moment how an idea developed in our own country would find its echo across the Atlantic, and become a watch-word even in the western wilds. How turning to *home* the people, imbued with reverence for all their fathers loved and lost, would carry on the cry till it found its echo in the deeds of the nation. And these very people, though individually of small account now, and of little influence, because the traditions they cherish are interwoven with old feuds and wrongs, and act as drags to their advancement, are the men of the future in America. To a vital energy which is unequalled, the Irishman unites an intellect which only requires to be directed by experience to make its influence felt, and an instinct of right and wrong almost poetical in its intensity. These powers will have an ample field for exercise in that great country, where the native Anglo-Saxon race is dwindling, and can never be restored to equal vigour by the new immigration from the East; and they will serve to counterbalance effeteness in the American, and want of principle in the Mongolian. And as it is a law, so far as we can judge from history, that the nobler qualities of a race manifest themselves despite all difficulty, this race – this leavening race of future America – this race which we young men may each of us directly and indirectly influence for good or ill, may become in time the leading element of Western civilization.

But not in America alone will Ireland manifest herself – abroad and at home alike will she make her influence felt. I have merely taken this example, because here the change is already in progress. Ireland in all her suffering of centuries has gained this one advantage – her people have remained the same whilst other peoples have slowly changed for the worse. And now amongst these others comes forth this old-world people – seeming half barbarous amid an age of luxury, but with strength and pride intact, and claims its position, as, at least, their equal. They in turn have had supremacy, but they have purchased it with their strength. There are no bad debts in races; and the purchase-money for greatness must sometime be paid. Her three hundred years of strife and idleness in which she has well nigh become a by-word to the nations, has strengthened Ireland for her future – the land has remained fallow, and the new crops will spring fresh and green. The Irish race has in it all the elements of greatness. Lord Byron's aphorism holds forth its hope – 'Out of chaos God made a world, out of high passions comes a people.' The very same individuality and self-assertion and passionate feeling which prompt to rebellion, and keep alive the smouldering fires of disaffection, become shrewdness, and enterprise, and purpose in commercial prosperity: and high spirit continues the same power in wealth as in poverty. Surely through all their sad career the courage and devotion of our countrymen have never yet been found wanting. In the midst of all her sorrow Ireland's hope has remained unshaken; and the valour of her sons has been proved in every great battle of Europe from Fontenoy to the Redan. Aye truly, at home or abroad, with the wisdom of education to guide her force, and the certainty of safety to secure her commerce, and to develop her resources, the Ireland of the future is a subject for ambitious dreams.

But the new order must be based on no sectarian feuds. The old animosities must be forgotten, and all the dead past left to rest in peace. There have been wrongs, but they are atoned for – there have been errors, but they are corrected – there have been insults, but they are wiped away. Is it wise to remember what to have suffered is our shame? Is it good for the cause of freedom that free men should treasure up the chains that bound their sires? If we are ever to be great we must forget that we have been little: if we are ever to be noble we must begin by generosity, and forgive what has long since been acknowledged as a wrong. It may be for us, to be the foremost men of the advancing race. We can choose whether we shall live for the future or follow the past; and it needs little effort to see the nobler choice. In our society we begin our lives as men thinking for ourselves, and every step is not indirect, but direct to the final end. But in our steadfast advance to that end we must not trust too much to belief in our cause. That belief is only the prompting to endeavour, but the action in obedience to it will be good. In learning to be just we shall not feel any immediate change, and the tenor of our lives will be much the same as ever. But when our course in this society is run we shall find ourselves passing out into the great world beyond our College gates, not bond men, but free: brave, because hopeful, – strong because incorruptible – steadfast because true. The world is for us as it has ever been for others, and the same purpose and the same labour which made them great will fulfil our ambition also. Time in its revolutions brings up new combinations every hour, and in the kaleidoscope of the world each change shows us something to learn. Races and nations rise and fall: systems of government make their votaries great, and then effect their ruin from too blind belief: schemes of polity spring up and flourish and decline. All time, and all place, and all action, blend finally into one vast union – the world renews itself again and again; but every change brings some increase of good. Everything sinks and falls in turn, and nothing is eternal but Truth and Progress. These are abiding principles which no force can stem or stay; but in hastening their glorious end we all can aid. We, here, a few young men, with traditions of the past to direct us, and the responsibility of guiding the future to make us prudent, may do much. We are young enough to hope – we are old enough to act – and in hope and action lies the future of ourselves, our country and our race.

13 November 1872
Trinity College, Dublin

PART 2

Theatre

Actor-Managers

(Part I. by Bram Stoker)

The growth of the system whereby actors have acquired the control of
the most important playhouses is simply a process of evolution. It
need not, I think, be hard to show that it is a matter of good effect not
only to those immediately concerned, and to dramatic artists, in general, but even, in greater or less degree, to literature and the arts, and
so to the great public.

The history of the Stage reflects the history of the Nation, and a
short view of the history of legislation on the subject may help us to
understand the process of devolution of stage power into the hands of
the players.

From the first in England, players seem to have been regarded
somewhat in the light of members of a craft or guild. Thus, in the
sumptuary enactments of Edward the Fourth and Henry the Eighth,
'Players in their Interludes' – the earliest allusions to them in the
statutes – are exempted from the penalties of wearing apparel not
allowed to their degree. In the early days of the creation of the English
Drama they were under the protection of the monarch or of great
nobles; and this protection, which was at first of certain service, was
practically a bar to the formation of any guild or mystery, so that they
were deprived of this form of aid to corporate advancement.

It was not until the fourteenth year of Queen Elizabeth's reign,
1572, that the first Act was passed which mentioned players in any
way constructively lowering to personal dignity. This Act related to
'Roges, Vacabonds and Sturdie Beggars,' but in its defining clause it
included players as follows: – 'common players in enterludes, and
minstrels, not belonging to any baron of this realme, or towards any
other honorable personage of greater degree;' or who 'have not licence
of two Justices of the Peace at the least, whereof one to bee of the
Quorum, where and in what shire they shall happen to wander.' That
the Act was not levelled specially at the Stage is shown by the list of
unlawful occupations also included in the Act: – 'unauthorized proc-
tors, gamesters, palmestrists, physnomists, bearwards, juglers,
pedlers, tinkers, counterfeiters, scholars of Oxford and Cambridge
begging without licence, shipmen pretending losses, and a such like
folk.' This law has been much misunderstood, for it treats purely of
vagrants, being merely a re-enactment of former statutes from the time
of Edward the Third down, and applies only to those itinerant players
who have not complied with the conditions laid down as necessary. A
decree of the Sovereign and Council in 1556 prohibited strolling players

through the country, whereas this Act gives greater freedom and provides for proper licences from those able to enforce protection and to accept responsibility. This power of licensing was, by an Act of 1598, afterwards amplified as follows: 'common players in enterludes and minstrels not belonging to any Baron of this Realme, or any other honorable Personage of greater Degree, to be auctorized to play, under the Hande and Seale of Armes of such Baron or Personage,' &c. Some five years later this power of licensing by nobles was taken away by an Act of James the First.

The vagrant statutes, however, although they were in various ways amended during the reign of nearly every successive monarch so as to follow in some degree the growing enlightenment of the age, continued the proviso against strolling players 'not being duly authorized by law' down to 1822. In this year was passed the last statute in which even strolling players are mentioned as rogues and vagabonds *in posse*; for before two years were over a new vagrant law had been enacted in which they are not mentioned. Though the inclusion in the statutes of players as rogues and vagabonds, when lacking legal authority, lasted for some two centuries and a half after 1572, the only unsatisfactory mention which I can find of them is in a marginal note to the Act 1 James I. c.7. Here the Statute of 1598, made against rogues and vagabonds in general, is referred to as follows: – 'Recital of Stat. 39 Eliz. c.4, §2, declaring Players, &c, to be Vagabonds:' it seems as if it was intended to convey that the recited Act had been made primarily against players, whereas in this very Act of 1598 the *ipsissima verba* of the Act of 1572 are used, whereby unlicensed players are only included amongst a crowd of other delinquents.

As time went on, however, the bounds of dramatic effort became enlarged, and players and theatres were sufficiently numerous to require some special enactment to duly regulate their undertakings. This came in 1736, with the Act under the elephantine title: – 'An Act to explain and amend so much of an Act made in the Twelfth year of the Reign of Queen *Anne*, intituled *An Act for reducing the Laws relating to Rogues, Vagabonds, sturdy Beggars, and Vagrants, and sending them whither they ought to be sent*, as relates to common Players of Interludes.'

The passing of this Act marks a change in theatrical history. Hitherto the only statutes affecting players had been the Vagrant Laws, with the exception of the early sumptuary enactments above mentioned, and an Act of James the First, forbidding profane language on the stage. These Vagrant Laws had always had some sort of economic or utilitarian basis, and had been enacted and re-enacted, enlarged or modified, to suit the exigencies of the time – the strolling players seeming to only share the lot of certain other wanderers from having been originally included in the comprehensive description of rogues and vagabonds given in the Act of 1572, and to owe their disability to neglect of legal obligations. The Act of 1736, however, lays down the law regarding actors as such, and states the penalties to which they may be subject for non-compliance with the laws thus made. The following provisions ruled the position of actors, for more than a century afterwards: –

'That from and after the 24th June, 1737, every Person who shall for Hire, Gain, or Reward, act, represent, or perform, or cause to be acted, represented, or performed, any Interlude, Tragedy, Comedy, Opera, Play, Farce, or other Entertainment of the Stage, or any Part or Parts therein, in case such Person shall not have any legal Settlement in the Place where the same shall be acted, represented or performed, without Authority, by virtue of Letters Patent from His Majesty, His Heirs, Successors, or Predecessors, or without Licence from the Lord Chamberlain of His Majesty's Household for the time being, shall be deemed to be a Rogue and a Vagabond within the Intent and Meaning of the said recited Act, and shall be liable and subject to all such Penalties and Punishments, and by such Methods of Conviction, as are inflicted on or appointed by the said Act, for the Punishment of Rogues and Vagabonds, who shall be found wandering, begging, and misordering themselves within the Intent and Meaning of the said recited Act.'

This Act of 1736,with an enlargement in 1787, continued in force up to 1843. An Act passed in this year still controls the management of theatres, subject to certain structural powers of the Metropolis Management Acts.

Briefly, then, the great Acts of Parliament affecting players were: (1) the Act of 1572 (14 Eliz. c.5), which included them, if not under the protection of a patron or licensed by the justices of the shire, as rogues and vagabonds: (2) the Act of 1598 (39 Eliz. c.4), which carried on this idea, having been accepted in successive reigns up to 1824; (3) the Act of 1603 (1 James I. c.7), which abolished the privilege of great nobles to give licences; (4) the Act of 1736 (10 George II. c.28), which recognised the existence of proper theatres, provided for the licensing of plays, and regulated the responsibilities of actors; and, (5) the Act of 1843 (6 and 7 Vict. c.68), which at present fixes the law on the subject.

Of course there have been other official ordinances besides statutes on the subject of theatres and players, but I have taken the Statute Book as the ultimate expression of the general tone or tendency of the law. There have been licences of the sovereign and great nobles, patents, royal warrants, and decrees of the Privy Council, and the Lord Chamberlain acquired certain powers under the common law; but all such were special exercises of power, and had some immediate purpose or motive in connection with individuals. It is in the laws made for all that we must find the general attitude of authority.

Let us, therefore, look at facts outside the Statute Book, and we shall see that all through the three centuries in which the Drama has flourished, public opinion has been almost invariably with the player, and not with the law, wherever and whenever it hampered the free development and exercise of the player's art. We shall see, moreover, that as public opinion became a more and more important factor in the government of the State, so such enactments became neglected, until they faded naturally out of the public view and became mere records of the existence of erroneous policy. Thus, certain statutes, whilst re-enacting the old laws, declare, not only by inference but even in words, that the previous law having fallen into disuse it now becomes necessary to enforce it, and so forth. Thus, again, theatres became organised despite the monopoly of patent houses, granted by Charles the Second, as when the theatre in Goodman's Fields was started without the necessary authority. When, in 1741, the two patent theatres remained empty through the rush to see Garrick, then commencing his great career, it was by a threat of appeal to the law that the manager was compelled into a compromise, and Garrick joined Drury Lane. Again, the Act of 1736, which professed to rule theatres absolutely, enacted, amongst other matters, that no theatre should be erected anywhere except in Westminster or its Liberties, or where the King might be in residence; but with the growth of the population this clause became so near being a dead letter, that theatres sprang up in many places in defiance of it, just as the demand for them arose, and certain temporary licences by local justices were empowered by an Act of 1787 (28 George III. c.30). We may find another instance in the growth of the music-hall system, which has gradually attained such colossal proportions. At first these places of entertainment were merely dancing houses, whose character was such that they caused the passing of the Act of 1747-51 (25 George II c.36). As time went on their number increased, and greater privileges were allowed them, until the present draft Bill of the London County Council allows them all the privileges of theatres proper, as to the production of stage plays. The reason, then, for this wide difference between the theory of protection and restraint, as expressed all along in the laws, and fact, as exemplified by daily life, was that the art was acquiring greater dignity, and the players were achieving a higher status amongst their fellow-citizens by degrees: the exercise of the art helped in many ways to advance the artists. At the start, the players were worthy people enough, some of them having acquired wealth and honour; but as under the Stuart dynasty the age of grosser luxury flourished, so they often fell into the common errors of the time. It would be too much to expect that one class should be free from common vice, but yet we find that the stage was never without some great actor whose worthy life was an example to his time. Betterton succeeded Burbage, and was followed by Wilks. Garrick was succeeded by the Kembles, Young, Macready, Phelps, Charles Kean, and so on to our own day. Indeed, if we take the succession of actors from Shakespeare down, we fairly find that the one who was crowned by public favour wore the golden circlet of his own kingdom quite as worthily as even the Monarch of the State in succession. It is in this very fact of public favour that we find the rationale and the genesis of the actor-manager. The public has its own discrimination; and its judgment, being the resultant of varied needs and interests and wishes, is sure to be in the main correct – *vox populi vox Dei* has a basis of truth which wise statesmen and students of men do well to consider. Public favour, when bestowed on a producer of work of any kind, is a valuable commodity; and to a player it is especially valuable, since his work is purely personal and cannot be reproduced or multiplied; like literature or music or work in the plastic arts. Thus, when the player has won his place, fortune follows, and his power can be turned into wealth, influence, position – that which he may aim at and which it is in him to achieve. Why, then, should he not use this power in the best direction and in the manner most serviceable to himself? Actors could have early used their power to this advantage, but that the road was barred on the one hand by the system of patronage or by patents which limited the number of theatres, and, on the other, by the laws which deemed them, if not under protection or licence, rogues and vagabonds. In the seventeenth century this double disadvantage was prohibitive of any effort at advance, for the actors were few, there was no system of provincial theatres at all, and the Court party, to which the subservient patentees belonged, was all-powerful. But with the growing liberties and larger population of the eighteenth century, things began to mend. In spite of the Vagrant Laws players travelled about, though in but a rough way enough, and new theatres which arose in spite of the patents were in time recognised even by the authorities.

The system of actor-management grew with the times. The foremost and most progressive managements have always been those of actors; and to-day nearly every theatre in London where serious plays are seriously produced under wholesome and permanent conditions is thus managed. That the fact is one worthy of the time is manifest; and when we come to think that though in London, with its many theatres, there are only a very few whose work is known to the great world, and that these are nearly all managed by actors, it is not hard to estimate that the actor-managers must exercise an enormous influence on the dramatic art of the time. It would be a strange policy, indeed, to strike off, in the cause of art, the heads of these taller poppies in its garden.

I have already explained how to a player popularity becomes a valuable stock-in-trade or capital, which only requires to be properly used to become realisable. This form of incorporeal property can of course be used by others than its immediate possessors – as, for instance, when such a one parts with some of his monetary capital in the shape of fixed salaries to popular artists; but manifestly the successful player can do best for himself by dealing at first hand with the public, if his capacities and opportunities allow of such an effort. He is certainly wise in making the trial, if he is satisfied that his prospects justify the risk, and if he have in hand sufficient capital of the more material kind to meet such engagements with others as it is necessary to make. He may be sure that if there were not at least some possibility – if not probability – of great reward, the middleman himself would hardly be willing to take the risk. A manager must have some attractive personality in his theatre. No matter how good the play or how complete and pleasing its environment, there cannot be success without good players. The successful actor, therefore, who goes into management, starts with one great attraction – his own reputation with the great public.

Of course the actor who would thus capitalise his popularity and become a manager, without ceasing to be an actor, should first be assured of the support of the public. This is best shown by the public approval of what he has already done. 'It is germ of the future,' says Cousin, 'which history seeks in the past.' No man can become a favourite of the public without the possession of qualities on which such favour can he based; and the public taste is constant. Though it may take years to achieve a place in public favour, when once that place has been won it is seldom indeed that it is lost, unless it be forfeited through misdoing. The player, then, who aspires to management under such almost assured conditions, may fairly calculate on the limited amount in the world of true artistic worth, and may feel himself fortified in his purpose by the words of a great writer when touching on the subject of art-intellect: 'You have always to find your artist, not to make him; you can't manufacture him, any more than you can manufacture gold. You can find him, and refine him; you dig him out as he lies nugget-fashion in the mountain-stream; you bring him home; and you make him into current coin, or household plate, but not one grain of him can you originally produce.'

Let us now, acknowledging the fact that actors have become managers, and with some understanding of how they have achieved the position, consider of what value are the arguments which have been of late advanced against the wisdom of the system. It has been asserted that the reign of actor-managers is responsible for the following: – (1) the exclusion, through personal jealousy, of players of superior excellence; (2) excessive expenditure on the mounting of plays to the starving of the outlay on the company; (3) the acceptance of inferior plays when suitable to the idiosyncrasies of the manager; and (4) an insufficiency of new plays.

First, then, as to the jealousy which excludes good actors. The charge when made is a general one, and, so far as I have found, is unsupported by a single instance of any kind: therefore, as it cannot be refuted in detail, the answer must be a general one. Let it suffice that the same cry has always been made, and will always continue so long as there are inferior artists. The same charge was made against Garrick, and yet hear the comment of Dr. Doran: 'I know of no proprietor of a theatre, himself an actor, who collected around him such a brilliant brotherhood of actors as Garrick did; yet, when any of these left him, or was dismissed by him, the partizans of the retiring player raised a cry of "jealousy!" ' He played with Smith, Bensley, Yates, and Palmer; he had in his company both the Barrys, and when he heard of the excellence of Mrs. Siddons's acting he engaged her also. Kemble engaged George Frederick Cooke for Covent Garden, and played Richmond to his Richard, and Antonio to his Shylock. Macready, when he heard of Phelps, then a country actor making a mark, wrote to an intimate friend to engage him for his company – not because he was jealous of him, but because the newcomer was reputed a good actor. The same anxiety to get good actors in actor-managed theatres is to-day in existence, although more intensified, because the growth in the number of the theatres is greater in proportion than is the increase of popular actors; and yet the cry still continues. Let the charge, then, be refuted entirely by a journalistic utterance made but recently regarding the engagement of a company for the next season of a London theatre: 'The company is one of the most powerful that could be brought together. This is well for the theatre; but for the public it has its drawbacks … It will be much to have one play peerlessly acted; but the theatres generally will be placed under contribution for its excellence.'

We may well ask, Where are the good actors who 'never get a chance' through jealousy or from any other cause? A very little examination of the facts will throw a somewhat sad light on the subject, for the unsuccessful ones will be found to fail from some defect of their own in the way of conduct, of self-value, or of personal equipment suitable for the task which they have undertaken. We must not accept a man as justly aggrieved because the world does not take him at his own valuation. Only a year ago there was a meeting of a large body of unemployed actors. They set forth their grievances, which the press duly recorded, and a committee was formed. A small body of some half-dozen actor-managers sent for the committee of the unsuccessful and asked them what they wished for. Their answer was to the effect that they wanted a chance of doing something for themselves, and of managing a theatre in their own way. The managers then and there gave them the sum of money which they said they would require. The experiment was made: they took a theatre and produced plays. In a very few weeks the whole organisation collapsed – there were internal dissensions, mutual recriminations, and unpaid balances. The scope of the effort was, it is true, humble, but it was sufficient to afford an object-lesson in theatrical management. The effort failed, although the adventurers were actors – the elements of their failure were perpetual. There is no royal road to success in theatrical management. The matter is a business which must be conducted in a suitable manner and with due knowledge; and as a skilled actor is more or less of an expert in stage matters the probability of his success is greater, *coeleris parabis*, than that of a less skilled person undertaking the same venture.

The second allegation concerning excess of decoration, to the detriment of the salary list, is best met by the simple fact that since the number of theatres has increased – the leading ones coming into the hands of actors – salaries of capable players have, on the average, nearly doubled. The young people of promise now get, at almost the very start of their working lives, larger salaries than were formerly obtained by players on the hither side of greatness. It is hard to believe, in view of current salaries – even taking the relative value of money then and now into consideration – that Garrick, with London in a *furore* at his phenomenal success, got only a salary of £600 per annum – twenty per cent greater than was ever before given to an English actor; that Mrs. Siddons came to Drury Lane at £5 per week; and that Edmund Kean, when the public fought for admission to see him play, had his salary *raised* to £20 per week. In the face of such facts as are within the knowledge of every person in connection with the stage or concerned in the management of a theatre, it is actually absurd to say that the salary list suffers because the production is complete. On the contrary, the perfection of one aspect of a play as given shows up any weakness that may exist elsewhere in it, and in every actor-managed theatre in London to-day it will be found that small parts are, almost of necessity, played by a class of capable actors which a few years ago could only have been found in the second or third ranks of the cast.

Thirdly, any question of the influence of the system of management under consideration on the play-writing of the time touches both the acceptance of plays by managers and the material in the shape of new plays annually produced. The statement that managers only accept plays which suit their individual capacities as actors is really hardly worth serious consideration. Of course a manager only accepts plays suitable to his company, if the company is made up before the play is accepted; and it must not be forgotten that in actor-managed theatres the manager is presumably, at the least, one of the best actors in the theatre, and that, consequently, in the selection of plays the fact has to be borne in mind. It would be silly for any manager to accept a play which could not be properly performed, and, indeed, the first person to object to such a thing would be the author, who would thus see his work imperilled. It is actually now a custom with some authors, when arranging for the production of their plays, to retain the right of a veto on the cast. A manager committed for a season to one company cannot profitably engage another; economic requirements must, as a rule, restrain such business arrangements. When a good play is nowadays accepted, a company to suit it is engaged; but this is done at a time and in a manner to suit the policy of the management and the length of its purse. Were a manager to refuse a good play simply because parts in it were too good for others of his company to suit his own vanity, the result of such unworthy and suicidal action would not be uncertain. The house so divided against itself would soon fall.

Fourthly, with regard to the alleged insufficiency of new plays, it must not be forgotten that even dramatists and actors are not always of one mind with regard either to plays or characters in them. Indeed, the statement may be made more general, for many a literary work when subjected to the opinion of a third party does not meet the reception expected by its author; there is not an editor in the world who has not experienced this. Of course, the judgment may err – even an experienced actor may fail to realise the worth of a play; but as it is the aim of the manager to get good plays, and of the actor to get good parts, surely when both conditions have to be fulfilled, the result must be manifestly better plays, though the excluded ones may be more numerous and the judgment more captious than before. But the fact remains that under actor-management good plays increase, and lacking it they decrease. From the time Garrick ceased to manage Drury Lane the production of plays declined. Moreover, there never was a time with regard to the immense output of plays like the present, when the system complained of is in vogue; so that we can only wonder at the abysmal ignorance which underlies the charge. Roughly speaking, from an average of the past few years, a new play of some sort or another is produced for each working day of the year in England, though out of these there is not one, on the average, in each month which makes a success – either financially or *d'estime*. During the good months of the year in London, new plays are produced in large numbers. Certain theatres are conducted with regard to matinées for the purpose; plenty of capable actors are always available; stage managers with all the requisite knowledge abound, and costumiers are ready to supply dresses at reasonable cost. There is then no possible difficulty in any author having a play produced on his own account; and a good play when once produced will not have long to wait for a purchaser, or for some manager who will pay fee or royalty. If his wishes and aims be modest the author can easily fulfil them, for, even if he have no capital of his own wherewith to pay expenses, he may obtain the help required by the ordinary method of poor inventors. Where, then, is the difficulty? For what part in the great negative result complained of is the actor-manager responsible? I fear that the answer is too sadly simple to please the carpers. Actor-managers, as a rule, know their business, and they will not produce bad plays. Too often the seeker after dramatic honours is not content to avail himself of the means of testing his work open to all. He wants to secure the services of the best artists and to have all done under the most favourable conditions; and he would pick a theatre whose record is such that the public will accept the work of its manager blindfold – partly, indeed, because that manager does not produce anything which is not good. If such manager will not see sufficient merit in a play to warrant its production, the writer is aggrieved. Not long ago Mr. Irving put the matter in a nutshell. 'We are told,' he said, 'that if we do not produce abundance of new plays, we crush the rising dramatist; whereas, if we do produce them, the rising dramatist crushes us!' Let any man bring with him a name already made famous in any branch of art or letters, or of professional or public life, and he will readily be granted a special consideration, for he has something to bring into the venture in addition to the work, whose intrinsic worth is unknown. But such men as this never complain. In fact, the unknown aspiring dramatist wants too much; he wishes to share, without any risk or equivalent whatever, a part of the fortune or distinction which other men have won for themselves. It seems *prima facie* unfair to ask that the manager, whose position has been partially assured by discretion in his choice of work, should imperil his acquisition by a divergence, without adequate cause, from his habitual policy. It is, of course, not a pleasure for any man to thwart budding genius, or even to disappoint springing hope; but the serious matter of any business must be considered in its proper place and sequence.

As to the influence of the control of theatres by actors on the other arts there is nothing to argue, for the complaint is made by the modem critics themselves that the stage is overladen with scenic effect. This same charge has been in existence ever since the very dawn of the English Drama. It was made even in Shakespeare's time. It was made against Betterton, and was, perhaps, justified in the worst days of Charles the Second, when, for instance, he contributed £500 for robes for the performance of *Cataline*. It was made again when Garrick introduced costumes which he thought suitable to the play represented, and gave a large salary to Loutherbourg as his scene-painter. Later still it was made against Macready, when Clarkson Stanfield and David Roberts lent the aid of their genius to stage effects. Charles Kean's name became almost a by-word through a persistent body of detractors, who called him 'the upholsterer.' That there is large expenditure on the appointments of a modern production is manifest, and that the arts benefit thereby is equally apparent. From time to time some of our best painters and composers are engaged in work for theatres. Alma

Tadema, Marcus Stone, Seymour Lucas, Edwin Abbey and Keeley Halsewelle, Sir Arthur Sullivan and Dr. Mackenzie are amongst the instances. Beyond this, again, literature itself owes much to the Stage and the player. Some writers have derived incalculable benefit from the suggestions and the help of the actors, and have not hesitated to say so, as when Sir Edward Bulwer Lytton handsomely acknowledged the great services rendered him by Macready. Many plays would not have been successful when produced, or would never have been produced at all but for the changes made by the players; and when these have, as managers, power to carry out their ideas, surely the benefit must be increased. Is it, then, to be said, or even thought, that the professors of the cognate arts have no advantage in the work done for the Stage – that the great world has no gain by another channel being opened, through which the head waters of genius can send streams to the great sea of man's higher labours? or can any one for a moment argue seriously that such example, followed at intervals proportionate to their powers, is not good for the rank and file of all the workers in connection with the various arts and crafts.

If any side light be required on the efficiency of the system of actor-management, let us look at the progress of other countries. The modern critics are perpetually quoting the French method as an exemplar in management. Certainly the Comédie-Française is a great corporation, and one which has done splendid work; but then in it the plays are selected by the actors. It requires, however, certain improvements to be effected. So long, also, as mere talent is held in corporate esteem without the discriminating admiration which the public has for genius, so long will the Rachels and Bernhardts and Coquelin secede from its ranks, unless accepted under their own conditions. The Germanic nations, too, which have a principle of subsidy in the Court and Stadt theatres, are beginning to find out that genius has an explosive force of its own. When we find already the best theatre in Berlin controlled by an actor – Barnay – we may well look for further development. Every system which works honestly can attain certain good, if not great, ends; but if we look for an ideal system of art development we must find it in some orders of things where individual freedom has a part, and where national life and opportunities admit of their adapting themselves to the growth. Some years ago a good many of the leading actors of the world met at a social gathering in London; it was a rare occasion, for there were English, Americans, French, and Germans. The opinion of almost every individual present was so interesting that conversation became formulated, and each took the torch in turn. Various opinions were expressed, but the most impressive amongst them was the comment of a great German actor: – 'State aid is good, subsidy is good, and in Germany and France the art of acting flourishes; but your English freedom is worth them all!'

It is in things theatrical as in all other affairs of life – put matter in solution and it will crystallise if such be its nature, or it will become a sediment in its own way. English freedom has, despite all troubles, evils, and mistakes, made England what she is, and has invariably worked out in time its own economic salvation. Why, then, should there be this one exception to all its rules? The natural result of power cannot be denied the men who have passed through the *Sturm und Drang* of artistic endeavour, and who by their knowledge and their gifts can, without losing touch with the people, help to direct public thought. No good object can be achieved by carping at natural laws which fix direction as well as strength in the resultant of multitudinous forces.

(Part II. by Henry Irving)

I entirely agree with those whose anxiety for the welfare of the stage would relieve actors from the cares of management, for I have often wondered how actors have ever been able to retain, as managers, the popularity which they may have won as artists, or why, experiencing the troubles of management, they have ever continued to hold the reins. In the exercise of their art, they are in some ways desperately handicapped, for a large portion of the time and labour which would almost insure artistic success is required by the needs of the purely business aspect of the undertaking. No one can know, except by personal experience, the worries to which a nervous or excitable manager can he subject; and when to this is added the fact that frequently actors have sacrificed in the vortex of management whatever fortune they may have achieved in the practice of their art, the surprise is not diminished. The small competence with which some of our greatest actors have retired was generally made after they had relinquished management. Thus, regretfully as Macready retired from the direction of Drury Lane – and his regret was almost equal to that of the public, whom he had so well and faithfully served – he was compelled to play engagements throughout the country, in order to realise some provision for his later years. Such, also, is the record of Charles Kean, Charles Mathews, Webster, Buckstone, Phelps, and others. It would certainly have been better for them if they had resisted the blandishments of management, and relied for their fortunes on their individual powers as actors. That the public would have been the losers I believe, for none know better than actors the value of a well-cast play, or are more willing to give to the public the full excellence which they can command. They, as artists, are generally more fastidious than others, and therefore more anxious for that thoroughness and completeness which they so well appreciate. The fitness of artists to deal with artists ought never to be called in question.

The charge of jealousy amongst actors is nothing – they simply share this quality with the rest of mankind A somewhat similar allegation is equally made against lay directors, who are now and again accused of favouritism.

It will be asked why actors should desire at all to be managers if the benefit of such labour is not mainly to themselves. The answer may be given that there are sometimes other and higher aims than the mere accumulation of money. Fortune may follow enterprise, but every artist does not make it the chief end or aim of his effort. He loves his work. What pleasure, for instance, can be greater than that of guiding the talent of younger people? Any effort in this direction is a public good. In a country where there is no Academy, the only professors of acting are the actors, and the only true school for acting is a well-conducted playhouse. For the first three years of my early stage life I had engagements at theatres then under the management of actors – Mr. Davis of Newcastle, Mr. Wyndham of Edinburgh, and Mr. Glover of Glasgow – and each of them took pleasure in imparting to the younger members of their companies, as well as circumstances permitted, some of their own stage knowledge and the rudiments of their art. I then spent some years in another theatre, under the management of a proprietor not an actor. During the whole of these later years I missed grievously the sympathy and advice of my old actor-managers, and I had to grope my way as well as I could without counsellor or friend. Such was my own experience of the system to which – as well as to the individuals – I owe a lasting debt of gratitude. I make no attempt to argue the question as to the right and proper people to become the managers of theatres. This is a matter which the public decide for themselves. I speak from an experience of over thirty years, and of this country only; and I can say, without hesitation, that the managements which have benefited and advanced our calling and added vastly to the intellectual recreation of the people have been those of actors.

Dramatic Criticism

The ultimate importance of dramatic criticism is shown in the amount of space allotted to theatrical matters in the journals of the day. It is the duty of newsmongers to supply the want of the public, and it may be fairly taken for granted that if there were no demand the supply, even if continued, would not have a perpetual growth. In both England and America there is on every great newspaper some official to whom is entrusted the collection and editing of theatrical news. In America this individual has a definite position as 'dramatic editor.' His work is aided, if not simplified, by the existence of the 'press agent,' now generally attached to every prominent theatre, who supplies to him items of interest presumed to be of importance by the advance agent of what is known as an 'attraction.' Thus it will be seen that in this great mass of theatrical material, chiefly composed of exchange matter, rumour, and gossip, there is a special need that the judgment set forth as that of the newspaper itself, through its experts, should be accurate and adequate. It is the critical little leaven which is to leaven the whole lump. This is not only possible, but easy, of achievement, since the multiplying of the necessary number of writers leaves the critic proper to attend to his own work, whilst the dramatic editor and his staff do all that may be required in the way of making straight the path of the coming players. In fact the critical Dr. Jekyll need have no connection with the rumour-bearing Mr. Hyde.

What, then, should be the equipment of a dramatic critic and his intellectual attitude whilst addressing himself to his task, it being taken for granted that he must obey all those rules which the experience of ages has formulated for the guidance of critics generally, whilst at the same time he gives special heed to those other rules, dependent on the *differentia* of dramatic as distinguished from other art?

Ordinarily a critic should have primarily a sympathetic understanding of the matter on which he sits in judgment:

> A perfect judge will read each work of wit
> With the same spirit that its author writ.

How much more necessary is this spirit when that which the critic reads is writ in tone and action on a page of passing emotion – all as swift and evanescent as a wind-sweep across still water. And yet there are here and there to be found writers, who take so harsh, so illiberal, or so jaundiced a view of their high calling that, to use Fielding's phrase, they construe the Greek word for criticism in its legal sense only – condemnation, instead of judgment. The arts are liberal, and from their very essence require not only a tolerant understanding of their aim and method, but a generous appreciation of even their less-er efforts and their minor issues. The world would be but a poor place after all were it not for the arts; and it is a poor art indeed which can-not tend toward the advancement of some ideal. That artist is indeed low down in the scale of human excellence whose labours do not brighten and beautify, or at least soften the harshness of things. Of all the arts, that of acting requires the most sympathetic understanding; for, though the means of its expression are of the subtlest, being through the exercise of the powers of God's last work – man, its hap-penings are so quick and so impalpable that before they can be well exposed to the influence of foreign judgment their very memory is temporarily obliterated by the exercise and purpose of succeeding emotions. It is here that some understanding of the actor's intention becomes of importance; for unless the judge either has some previous knowledge of it, or allows his own sympathy to move as freely as its subject, it can hardly be possible for him to grasp the idea of a consis-tent character working always through one individuality, and yet sub-ject to varied passions and emotions. But the dramatic critic has to study, follow, absorb not only one character under varying aspects and conditions, but each and every character in the play; so that if his brain be already loaded with theories, and if his sympathies be already choked with antagonistic purposes, he is little apt to arrive at that great truth, whatever it may be, at which the actor and the audience are conjointly aiming. In this matter of quickening sympathy the best lesson in criticism comes from the audience whose swift and accurate judgment is shown every now and again by the spontaneous cheer, which shakes the playhouse and justifies in a way the action of that gifted scribe who, crystallizing public sentiment, first turned enthusi-asm into an active verb. And yet there are instances of men who seem completely blind to the value of sympathy in criticism, and approach the matter in a seemingly hostile spirit. I know, for instance, of one dramatic critic – dramatic critic and translator of plays – either so per-versely stupid or so lamentably ignorant of the very first principles of his calling as to write thus: 'The actor, however little he may like to be told so, is a parasite upon the play.' If his statement were metaphysi-cally true, what a slur he, a critic, has cast by inference upon his craft; for if the actor be a parasite upon the play, what, in the name of logic, is the critic, who earns his bread or pursues his mission by writing of the actor?

Great fleas have little fleas upon their backs to bite 'em,
Little fleas have lesser fleas and so *ad infinitum*.

'It is a dirty bird,' says the old English proverb, 'which fouls its own nest.'

Again, the critic of the drama should have at least some special knowledge of the subject of his work, unless, of course, he be one of those gifted individuals whose omniscience is intuitive, or he have that which must not be expected of any man, a sufficient modesty to hide his own ignorance. For the dramatic critic has to judge not only the player, but the play! and a play is a mightily complicated piece of work. As it has to appeal to all or most of the senses, it has everywhere a bearing on some branch of human knowledge, since the eye has to be pleased and satisfied, beauty as well as accuracy has to be observed, and the production of a play in an educated age is no light task. In external scenes the flora of place and season have to be correctly given – the scene painter who knows his work must even study the characteristics of cloud and atmosphere. The historical period, the nationality, and the social degrees of all concerned have to be accurately shown; even the habits and bearing of an age and country are of importance. These things all mean very special study somewhere, and when painters and historians have carefully collaborated with management and actors, it requires a learned critic to be able either to fully appreciate or to justly condemn what is shown. The spread of archaeology has been mainly aided by the stage, for it has been by the wholesale setting forth of the environment of a period or an event that the great public has come to have familiar knowledge of such matters. In such a mass of material as a stage setting requires it is comparatively easy to find a flaw; but this is a very different thing from the conception of even a crude idea upon the subject. It is, I think, hardly too much to say that it will take the most superior judgment to be found in England or America to fitly and fully appreciate the work of a great play properly produced, so as to enable the writer to translate and point out its excellences to the vast body of the – incompletely – educated public.

Let me here say that, speaking with a considerable knowledge of dramatic criticism and dramatic critics in both England and America, I can bear willing testimony to their general worth. I have found them to be, as a body, earnest, liberal-minded gentlemen, sympathetic in their attitude toward the work, patient and fearless in their discharge of it, having no private purpose or end of their own to serve, but helping to enlarge the public sympathy and to purify the public taste by their appreciation of excellences and their condemnation of evil things.

So far, however, as we are informed, neither is there any special supply of heavenly fire to enlighten dramatic critics, nor are they or their body specially exempt from the evils that assail mankind. All callings have their less worthy or unworthy members, and the ranks of dramatic criticism have no special immunity from such. Further than this, it is probable that this body has more than its fair share of undesirable individuals, since there is no preliminary test of capability. The calling is an open one, needing necessarily no qualifications except the will of a newspaper proprietory. Thus there are to be found, here and there, fortunately at rare intervals, in the body of dramatic critics, as in all bodies, members of the criminal class, of the asylum class, of the hospital class – in fact of that class generally of cranks and faddists, whose place in the world of criticism is somewhat analagous to that occupied in the scheme of law by what are known as 'torts,' a class of civil offences, with a possible criminal bias. The distinctly criminal class is represented by a few individuals who are venal to the praise of unworthiness, and who have a blacker side of crime in that they extort, where and how they can, blackmail in money or in 'meal or malt' by either disseminating or withholding libel. These men are but few; and as they are pretty well known to every one in the theatrical and journalistic world, I cannot but think that an organized effort for their suppression by the men whose craft they sully would have an immediate and wholesome effect.

The critics of the hospital and asylum classes are harmless unless when they have some personal interest to serve, some spite to indulge, or some wound to their vanity to avenge: in such case, the pity which the reader of average intelligence has for them changes to a purposeful contempt. These cases are, however, rare; for as a rule the dramatic critic whose existence is built on vanity or *cacoethes scribendi*, or both, is harmless and is fully sheltered by the magnitude of his own incapacity.

Finally, the class of cranks or faddists includes certain varieties whose differentiation is a matter of almost entomological interest. The most common specimen is that of the 'provincial' writer. This individual is gifted with a sort of impregnable cocksureness, and to him nothing is hidden, for he reads the whole Arcana like an open book. His logic being of the purely feminine order – 'I think; therefore I know' – has to him no possible flaw, for his vanity supplies the blanks that his ignorance has passed, and his self-sufficiency covers up with a blinding glory all doubts as to fact. In some of the most intellectual centres of the English-speaking world such specimens are to be found, and it is to them that the word 'provincial' can be most suitably applied. 'Provincial' as an adjective is not geographical, but comparative. It implies a narrowness of vision or an intolerance of spirit tacitly taken to arise from inadequate experience. To eyes accustomed to the eternal passing of the great pageant of life the various items have only the importance of their place in the great scheme; but to eyes not so trained by habit each item seen by itself becomes of undue importance; and, inasmuch as lesser towns but seldom see these greater movements of the world, the opportunity of comparison does not exist in a measure sufficiently large to become of permanent educational value. Thus the comparison of a 'provincial' with a 'capital' view of things becomes instructive, we are enabled to fairly test the intellectual value of those who, though enjoying the opportunities of larger culture, find themselves – or rather are found by their readers – eternally limited by their provincial littleness. The work of a 'provincial' critic speaks for itself, and who runs may read the signs. For such a man loves to display his knowledge, and the sum of human knowledge is so great, and the amount of it which one person can acquire is so small, that the measure of his capacity can be gauged by the importance which he places on certain things which, though well known to others, are to him fraught with the weight of new acquirement. Thus, we may occasionally see an otherwise completely commonplace criticism speckled over with isolated chunks of the writer's previously disintegrated ignorance.

More commonly still one may notice comparisons made by such writers between existing things and others of which they are manifestly ignorant, and always to the detriment of the former. *Omni ignotum pro magnifico.* The most usual examples of this form of provincialism in dramatic criticism are those of comparison with foreign countries, as when American or British dramatic art is unfavourably compared with the glories of 'the French and German schools,' or when players of the day are held up as wanting in the excellences of the actors of the past – Garrick and Kean being the most commonly chosen examples, since they are well known names, and none living has seen them play. The purveyors of the foreign comparison are usually to be found in inland towns or cities, where they have had life-long residence, and they are generally as ignorant of the French and German tongues as they are of Tamil or Teluga. Those gifted beings who are enabled to raise the veil from the past or to evolve from their own inner consciousness the minutiae of the art of Garrick and Kean – and the methods of these two players probably embraced the whole cycle of histrionic art – are as a rule either very young men without either thought or experience, or else more hardened sinners in the ways of conjecture and in the vice of self-esteem. In either case they are manifestly in absolute ignorance of the principles, the aims, the limitations, the difficulties and the practice of the art upon which they sit in judgment. They simply draw upon their inchoate imagination for their nebulous facts. Any one with experience or knowledge of individual writers of dramatic criticism will recognize the justice of this description and easily identify, if such be worth while, the writers of this class.

As to the best method of achieving proper dramatic criticism on the part of those who are in all ways equipped for their work and perfectly unprejudiced in their desires, I should venture to suggest that in the case of a new play or an important revival of an old one the critic should not take as the field of his judgment the efforts of the first performance, when through the nervousness which is a necessary part of the artistic temperament many phases of effort are of necessity seen it their worst. He should wait until by a few repetitions the work of the various artists and operatives has been properly consolidated and smoothed. The occasion of a first performance is the opportunity for a descriptive reporter who can be eyes and ears to the reading public, rather than for the expert critic whose province it is to analyze and sit in judgment upon the play and the playing as seen by the great public during the progress of a run.

There is in the world no more honourable, no more responsible position for any man than to sit in judgment, and such an one should always feel the gravity and the weight of such an earnest task.

The Art of Ellen Terry

The place of Ellen Terry in the history of her art has been won by great gifts used with much skill and consistent effort. She has a power of pathos which passes beyond the bounds of art, and manifests itself as an endowment of especial excellence. The exercise of such a gift implies the existence of another quality – sincerity, for though art may not enable a person naturally without power to achieve a high place within its range, the want of it can deny to any one the reaching of its highest point, and in art the truth is all in all. The pregnant phrase of Pope, 'Nature to advantage dressed,' is an epitome of its scope and limitations. For art is not of necessity creative; its etymology shows that its purpose is rather to construct out of complete materials than to nucleate particles from the beginning. In fact, the word art, in its original meaning, 'to join,' shows that the artist is a joiner. An actor's work is both creative and artistic: but every expression of it given, beyond the first presentation, is of necessity purely artistic. It is achieved by means of an organised effort, carried out with intention, self-guidance, and restraint. Thus it is that what at times may seem a very whirlwind of passion, or an abyss of despair, is regulated and controlled by intention and by guiding principles as marked and definite as those which fix the bounds of the work of the painter, or the sculptor, or the architect. As the actor deals with the complex and varying emotions of humanity, his material is of endless variety; but still, even as the shape of humanity is fixed within certain lines, so that although individuals differ the type remains constant, so the work of the artist, although capable of an endless varying of expression, must remain within typical bounds. When this reticence is observed by an artist of any kind, his work is accepted critically as true, and exercises on those to whom it appeals the power which only truth and sincerity can achieve. Ellen Terry's early training had much to do with the development of her nature in her art. Sprung from a theatrical family, she was from the first in contact with the exercise of stagecraft. The youngest child may be drilled into imitative effort; but such effort must be in large measure consistent with natural emotion, or else the labour to both teacher and pupil is ineffective and evanescent. When she was very young, Ellen Terry made her appearance as Mamilius in *A Winter's Tale*, with a tiny triumphal car as a toy. It would almost seem is if nature in a mood of prophecy had thus typified the honours of her after-life.

In her earlier years she had a whole world of experience, and great artists like Mrs. Charles Kean took endless pains with her. Whilst Ellen was still a little girl, she and her elder sister Kate played as child-actresses with very considerable success. The experience thus gained in playing a range of parts otherwise impossible to her, served her in good stead later on in life; for though a child may not at the time understand to the full the words which it speaks or the emotions it may have to portray, the effect of the necessary study remains, and the fuller understanding comes with larger experience of life.

When as a very young woman Ellen Terry began to win her place with the public, her artistic charm seemed to have full scope and opportunity through her artistic training. She was not hampered at every turn by awkwardness incidental to a lack of knowledge of the differences of stage perspective compared with that of ordinary life. For it must never be forgotten that on the stage the measure of things is different from that in use off it. In fact, for critical accuracy there should be a quantitative as well as a qualitative analysis of stage fare. In the glare of the footlights and amid the surroundings, both implied and actual, of stage effect, the painter's perspective is sharper than that taught in the schools, and the 'vanishing-point' is closer to the beholder than it would be in a landscape. In a world where everything must be enlarged or intensified or concentrated to suit dramatic exigencies, ordinary conditions are out of place and do not seem true to Nature. Every art has its own necessary conditions. Art is not to *be* real, it is to *seem* real; and although the artist must understand the reality of things so that he may work to an ideal and, he must use the prototype as something to be represented rather than as something to be reproduced. In the mere matter of sound alone, the theatre requires a greater force than is necessary elsewhere under conditions of seeming similarity; an actor therefore must have a voice that can carry. Mere volume of voice is not sufficient; nor does it suffice that the method of speaking be cultured and natural. Both are necessary, if the deadening effect of a couple of thousand persons breathing in an opposite direction to the speaker is to be overcome. These mechanical difficulties must be mastered if success is to be achieved, and actors soon learn the limits of their physical powers. I do not know any better lesson for a young artist than to study Ellen Terry's method of delivery – such a speech as, for instance, Portia's 'Quality of Mercy' in *The Merchant of Venice*, or the little poem, 'Rainbow, Stay,' in Tennyson's *Becket*. In each of these, every condition of truth and fineness is observed as perfectly as though speaker and auditor were alone in a drawing-room; but there is a power behind the expression which amplifies and intensifies it indefinitely. From the stage there is a surprising volume of sound – sound articulated, modulated, varied with every thought passing through the speaker's mind, but still sufficient to fill the vast expanse of a theatre and penetrate to every corner of it, conveying all the while the minutest purpose of both the poet and his interpreter.

In every other way as well as with regard to sound, the requirements of the stage necessitate an enlargement of ordinary methods; and with all these the skilled actor must be thoroughly acquainted. These things are not to be adequately learned in a day, or a month, or a year. 'Art is long,' and it is, or should be, patient; for the lessons of it are endless. The performer on the stage must be so familiar with its needs, especially where these differ from ordinary life, that given a sense of environment, he will instinctively fit himself to his surroundings; and to this end time, and practice, and repetition are necessary. The mere technique is endless. For we must remember that on the stage it is not sufficient that the work be done in the round, like that of a sculptor. Every action, every pose, every gesture, every movement, has to be fitted to a condition of things which makes only one side of them visible; the whole of the routine of life has to be adapted to the conditions of a framed picture which can be seen from only one point of view. On the stage, while an actor is visible at all, the part of his body which can be seen is alone able to convey its lesson to the spectator's eye. In the old days when candles and oil-lamps did what they could to dissipate the gloom of a great playhouse, most of the actors, recognising the fact that without light they were lost, tried to arrange themselves in a row down on the footlights and there by face and gesture convey their intentions to the audience. But time and science have changed all this, and now the actor while 'on' has to be *en evidence* even though it be as a listener, or a sleeper, or a corpse; it is required of him that even at such times he shall be true to his part and do no violence to the essential conditions of these exemplifications of repose. When therefore we consider the extraordinary number and variety of conditions, sometimes antagonistic to natural surroundings, and sometimes differing from them in varying degrees, and when we remember that all these must be held in mind from first to last by the player, so that he may be able to force home illusion to the minds of the audience by counter-balancing the restrictions under which he works, we may get some idea of the manifold excellence of mind necessary for a great actor. Passion and coolness, purpose and premeditation, instinctive readiness to recognise and to conform to accidental conditions, all these are antecedent to success, and entirely exclusive of those creative and mimetic powers which go to form the personal equipment necessary for success. Through all these difficulties and studied differences Ellen Terry has held perpetually before her eyes the great exemplar, Nature, and each artistic end has been achieved by Nature's methods.

The range of her parts has been very wide, and she has won success in many fields. When, as the 'Wandering Heir' in Charles Reade's play founded on his story of the same name, she burst with all her charm upon the public, they thought that Peg Woffington had come again, for never had so winsome a girl become so fascinating a boy;

and when later on she played Olivia in Wills's version of *The Vicar of Wakefield*, she carried the pathos of tragedy into the sublime. Those – and they are many – who have seen her in the third act where Squire Thornhill unfolds to her the base story of his deception and her own betrayal, can never forget the ring of horrified amazement as she repeats the phrase, 'The truth?' or the chastened tone of her despair as, after striking him on his endeavouring to embrace her, she sinks back in her seat with the wail of self-regretting anguish, 'Lost – lost even my womanliness!' For this sweetness of disposition, even under terrible adversity, we are prepared from the outset of the play; the manifest sympathy between father and daughter can come only from hearts bubbling with light and love.

In the course of her artistic life Ellen Terry has played not only a great range of parts, but a great number of them, even exclusive of her early working years, when a young actor plays many parts of no special importance. It is by great work that an actor, or indeed any artist, is finally judged. When one person can play Lady Macbeth and Viola (*Twelfth Night*); Ophelia, Desdemona and Volumnia; Beatrice, Portia and Cordelia; Rosamund and Madame Sans-Gêne; Margaret, Nance Oldfield and Lucy Ashton, and can illuminate and adorn them one and all, each with its own suitable qualities and excellences, there can be no doubt as to her command of the resources of her art or as to the varying nature of her powers.

In some special characters she has made a place in art that is all her own – for instance, Iolanthe in *King René's Daughter* (re-christened *Iolanthe* in Wills's version) or Ellaline in Calmour's poetic play, *The Amber Heart*. In the former of these, her portrayal of the blind girl is full of delicate beauty; every touch and turn and word, every gesture and movement, is simply incarnate grace and sweetness. In the latter, pathos is carried to its limit; the sorrows of loss and the joys of gaining are exemplified with a depth of feeling which has more force with the imagination or the reason than fairy romance or the most argumentative of problem plays.

It is, however, in plays abounding in life that Ellen Terry has most personal delight. Her own nature here answers most willingly to the calls of her art. Her Beatrice, for instance, is a creature of vitality in whose veins run, together with the red blood, special corpuscles of fun. 'I was born in a merry hour,' she says to Don Pedro, and in almost every moment of her appearance during the play she makes her audience aware of the fact in a more eloquent way than by the speaking of Shakespeare's words. As should be in all good comedies, the effect of the fun or humour is brightened by a contrast, and a comedienne to be great must rise to the height of the larger emotions. In *Much Ado About Nothing* there is such a contrast, and this particular actress rises in it to a sublime height. The scene is where in the church her cousin is affronted by Claudio. Beatrice is full of generous rage at the baseness of the insult and of pity for the young girl so wounded to the heart. Burning with passion and weeping with compassion, she strides about the stage railing at Claudio's conduct and upbraiding Benedict for his tardiness of revenge; till finally her 'Oh that I were a man!' brings her bashful lover at once within the range of her love and her purpose of revenge. To see Ellen Terry play this scene is an enlightenment as to a woman's powers – of charm and passion, of pity and love, of cajolery and hate.

From *Much Ado About Nothing* to *Madame Sans-Gêne* is a far cry, and yet in both somewhat the same qualities are required. The age is different; the country is different – in fact, all the conditions of nationality, epoch, social quality, length of years, training, and equipment are varied; and yet such is the expression of essential womanhood in both that the grouping of these two characters well serves to illustrate the truth of Kipling's quaint phrase –

'The Colonel's lady and Judy O'Grady
Are sisters under their skins!'

An instance of the way in which the acting of a play grows may be taken from Ellen Terry's playing in *Madame Sans-Gêne*. At the first presentation of a play the characters are seldom so thoroughly elaborated as is afterward the case; familiarity with the part allows a competent actor to add to the minutiae, especially in such matters as belong to the differentia of the character. In the play in question, the washerwoman-Duchess is having a lesson from a professor of the choreographic art. The business of the play requires her to be awkward in her attempts at dancing, and the actress is awkward – delightfully awkward, with an assumption of ungainliness which to a naturally graceful woman must mean study and intention of no small degree. She has put on a long riding-habit in order to become accustomed to manipulate her court-train in the dance, and is so much troubled with it that finally she tucks it over her arm whilst she is learning how to take the steps. The train keeps slipping off her arm and has to be perpetually replaced, and the episode is a cause of much boisterous amusement. For many nights, both in London and the provinces, this scene was given without any change except such small matters as are necessitated by the accidents of the moment.

One night in a great manufacturing city she was playing the part with even more than her usual verve. She was lost in the assumed character so thoroughly that it was real to her, and the ex-washerwoman, with her mind harassed and worried by the trying conditions of her artificial court-life, instinctively returned to the habits of her youth. In a moment of abstraction, finding the fat coil of stuff across her arm, she instinctively began *to wring it out*. The response of the audience was electrical; every woman – and man – who had ever seen a washtub recognised the sincerity of the action. This moment of creative instinct was recorded in the actor's mind, and 'the business' – as in stage parlance anything is called which is not the words of the text – has ever since been repeated. This instance will convey a better idea than perhaps would be done by a more important episode of the dominating truthfulness to nature of the character and instinct of the great actress.

Another instance, the latest, of her sincerity to nature is given in her acting of Volumnia in Sir Henry Irving's production of *Coriolanus*. All great actors regulate their efforts so as to be consistent with their own personality; in an art of illusion it would be ridiculous to create unnecessary obstacles to the convincing of an audience.

Mrs. Siddons, for instance, who had quite other views as to the type of the character with which she had to deal, played Lady Macbeth as a dominating personality, ruling her husband with a rod of iron and compelling him to unwilling effort. She did this because she was of fine stature and commanding presence, with eyes that could blaze and features whose expression could be well seen even in the dim lighting of the playhouse of a century ago. Her Volumnia, too, was of the rugged, antique type, swaying her son's grim purposes with a larger dominance. Throughout, she commanded so effectively that her stooping to beg justified the comments of her son. In this character her nature and her physique were at home; there was equal poise for both the actress and the woman, From the records, we can judge that the inflexibility of the Roman matron was conveyed by her very presence; and it is certain that at the time her method was effective. To her dark, imperial beauty, personal dominance was almost a natural attribute, and she used it throughout so effectively that from beginning to end there was no soft spot manifest in her nature. Even Volumnia's love for her proud son was based rather on her own pride than on the joy of motherhood, and in the hands of Mrs. Siddons this singleness of nature always stood out to its full worth.

But *autre temps autres moeurs*. The century which has gone has given woman a truer place in the organisation of the world than existed at its dawn, and with a wider tolerance of woman's ambitions and efforts comes a better understanding of her limitations. Neither women nor men of to-day expect a strong man to take orders, no matter how imperiously the orders are given. 'Sweet reasonableness' has a part in the incitement to action, and especially in the persuasion to change.

For this reason, as well as to suit her own ideas and purposes, Ellen Terry has given us a different Volumnia. Without altering in meaning a single word of Shakespeare, she has vitalised his creation with her own nature. Her Volumnia is all woman; not weak woman, but woman in all her essential attributes. She has recognised that the force of such a mother was in her silence as well as in her speech; in the sweetness and common-sense of her domestic life as the mistress of a great household, as well as in those moments of haughty ambition in which she urged her great and victorious son to still greater and more victorious deeds. The ending of the author is attained in each case, but by means differing as widely as the personalities of the two actresses. When we see Ellen Terry sitting in her household as a true woman must, interested in the small affairs of daily life, and, after the manner of antiquity, dominating her son's wife even to gentle chiding of her fears, we realise that this is a woman who, when she does speak, will speak to some purpose. This reading of the character is essentially true to human nature, and in its sincerity has much, and added, force in the play. When Coriolanus listens, either to her upbraiding or her beseeching, he knows that the origin, and source, and cause of it are true; and it is this feeling pushed home to the hearts of the audience, as well as to the stage character, that saves the great Roman from an instinctive judgment of vacillation on the part of those who note in more than one instance the quick abandonment of his settled purpose.

Ellen Terry's education had a fortunate beginning. Though the lessons which a child learns at a very early age are but rarely retained in its mind as guiding principles, they are nevertheless of value if begun along natural lines. She never had to be forced to act a part or drilled to the point of fatigue, as is the case with many children. Her parts came naturally to her, and she never departed from the truth as she felt it to be in her portrayal of even the most conflicting emotions.

Indeed, the more we know of her method of stage art, both as to the conception of a character and the instinctive recognition of its place in the perspective of the play of which it is a part; of the sincerity of her regard for the essential truthfulness of things; and of the becoming and enchanting manner in which she can convey the purpose of her mind to the senses of her audience through all the resources of a subtle and vastly various art, the more we feel that her success and honours have been justly won.

The Question of a National Theatre

The idea of a National Theatre is at first glance an attractive one. The arts which cluster round the drama are arts which all men love, and each of which has individually established claims for respect and consideration far beyond the mere faculty of giving pleasure. One and all they can be, and are, of great educational value, teaching the power and worth of organisation in very high forms. Music and the plastic arts generally – all arts and crafts which deal with form and colour, are willing to assist in the development of dramatic form. This has been the gift of several ages; that which high civilisation has won in one phase of strenuous effort at advance. If, then, all the arts can be united in some formal and continuous manner so as to create a veritable temple of arts dedicated to human profit and worthy delight, the possibility of an effort to effect this is surely well worthy of consideration.

So far, this is true in principle. It applies to the drama and the theatre; it is only when we try to localise it that trouble begins. In an enlightened age like our own it is too late to begin to consider ethical values in the matter. It is apparent to all who have eyes to see and minds to understand that the theatre is an existing fact and that it has come to stay. But we are now in the stage when the direction of its working is still within our power. Drama and theatre have each educational possibilities for good or ill; it is for us to discriminate and to help. This can best be done by countenancing publicly that which is worthy; the exercise of *force majeure* is but a poor device in the government of the free.

For more than three hundred years we have had in this country a worthy drama and many good theatres controlled by worthy men – drama and theatres with high aims and lofty self-respecting ideas of their own values in the domains of art and thought. Beginning a century and a half later, but running synchronously since then, has been another form of entertainment, without the lofty art-aims and devoted to personal rather than organised effort. The time is coming fast – if, indeed, it has not already come – when the guardians and supervisors of State discipline will have to make some sort of choice between these two classes of public amusement. Such must – and probably shall – be shown in approval of one rather than in disapproval of the other; an estimable acceptance rather than a ban. As such approval must take some recognisable form, expressing itself either in material shape or honourable recognition, if not in both, it may be as well to consider in good time what must some day be thought over. For this purpose let us consider the question at present in the air through a strenuous setting forth by a few newspapers and many clamant personalities: that of a National Theatre. The occasion of this setting forth is in connection with the World's Memorial to Shakespeare, to which end a powerful committee has been at work for some three years or more. Those who have been persistently calling out for a National Theatre for quite a number of years past have, naturally enough to them, seized the occasion for making the claim on behalf of the memory of the great poet. How they can explain in what way Shakespeare is to be specially honoured by the realisation of a scheme which they hold to be required for other reasons, is a little difficult for ordinary people to understand. But, be this as it may, let us consider the idea of a National Theatre on its own merits and without reference to honouring anyone, however great.

The idea must be of an actual physical theatre – a place for producing and acting plays under the most favourable conditions; a theatre in the abstract means absolutely nothing whatever. A theatre is by its very nature one of the most concrete and practical workshops in the world; it is a place for *doing* certain things, and for the purpose must be as real as the life of which it is a part – civic or national, as may be. It is in fact a theatre built and aided or supported by some external power and with some resources outside itself. Ordinarily speaking, a theatre is supported by its own efforts. Some capital – or credit which can take the place of capital – may be required at first; but in the long run it must stand or fall by its own work. The plea, therefore, for a supported theatre can only be put forward on the ground that it may be of some special service in the organisation of public life; that it can supply something impossible under ordinary commercial and individual conditions. Granted, then, that such an institution might be of some direct service, the questions to be considered are: how far such an undertaking might fulfil its objects, and at what cost it could be organised and maintained. All things are relative, especially in statecraft, and where we are still so far off ideal perfection in the fulfilling of public needs and the organisation of public life the price of commodities for public use is an all-important and unavoidable question.

As to price, then, the requirements and necessary conditions of a National Theatre should be shown in howsoever a rudimentary way, so that students of the subject may form some estimate of the eventual cost. In the first place, as to the theatre itself. This being a national matter must naturally be placed in the national capital – in this case, London. It should be in a prominent and central position; it would not serve its purpose if placed in a back street or in a suburb. It should be of such dimensions and elevation as to serve in some sort as a monument of taste worthy of the nation which in its own way it represents. It should serve as an accredited model for all lesser and local enterprises dedicated to workings of a similar kind, with regard to safety, hygiene, resources, convenience, ease, comfort, elegance, and good taste – in all ways a model and exemplar of what should be and is capable of achievement. Thus it would set a standard – a series of standards – of excellence in many ways which would eventually tend to public good, and would thus justify its creation. Again, in its working it should show similar perfection, similar excellence in the adaptation of means to accepted ends. If such a theatre did not observe these requirements, what possible purpose could it serve? It would be merely one more theatre amongst a whole crowd of others; an eleemosynary undertaking upborne by external resources and thus unfairly competing against similar industrial enterprises unsubsidised in any form.

Granted, again, that such a theatre so conducted would make for public good, let us count the probable cost.

Such a theatre should cover a large space. A small theatre would be of no use; and, besides, we have already in London alone some three score of theatres, most of them of inconsiderable size. It should be large, so as to contain those who, as parts of the nation, must be considered in some respect its owners; and again, as prices should be cheap, so as to give facilities to poor as well as to rich, it would take a large auditorium to hold a sum compatible in some degree with the necessary expenses. In addition there should be ample space for plenty of staircases, passage-ways, crushrooms, cloakrooms, offices, billrooms; in fact room for all the proper and decent, not to say commodious, working of a large establishment employing a vast number of hands. Those who are not familiar with theatres would be astonished to know the number of persons employed in a large theatre. For instance, in the management of the old Lyceum Theatre Henry Irving employed as many as six hundred persons of one kind or another; the number seldom if ever ran below four hundred and fifty. Again, on the stage side there is to be considered not only the stage – which for such a theatre, where frequent changes of bill would be expected, should be of very considerable size – but room to store away and take out with facility much scenery, properties and wardrobes. Much space would also be needed for dressing-rooms, green-rooms, and sanitary appliances for many people of either sex. Also a good many workshops, for such matters as demand instant attention. All these requirements mean great space, and in London space in a prominent centre – and especially large space – means great money. For instance, when the Strand widening began and the southern side of the thoroughfare was thrown back, where the entrances to the Savoy and Cecil hotels now are, the ground behind the houses at the eastern end was sold at what the appraisers called 'eight shillings a foot.' This, at thirty years' purchase, which was the arrangement announced, worked out at £12 per foot. It may convey some idea of the value of land when I say that the freehold of the old Lyceum – no 'hinterland' remember, but a space surrounded on three sides by thoroughfares – would have worked out to a capital value of some £250,000 or £300,000. The area of the old Lyceum, though covering a good space, would not be nearly large enough for the erection of a proper 'National' Theatre.

The building, too, of such a theatre would be a costly affair, for such, as representing a phase of the ambition of a great and wealthy nation, should be worthy of it. The mere size and stability of structure necessary to achieve safety and comfort would alone be costly; the architecture and handsome material of construction might represent any sum within the bounds of reason. In any case, it would not be possible to acquire such a space and to erect an adequate theatre on it for a less sum than half a million of British money.

Then as to the working. There is no comparison at all between the expenses of a big and a small theatre. Such is not a mere matter of multiplication. Size is in itself a matter of cost and brings with it a host of collateral expenses. As a National Theatre should be of standard excellence, the expenses would necessarily be greater than are required for one conducted by private enterprise and with naturally limited means. It may afford, however, some basis for estimating expense if I give some approximate details of expense of working the old Lyceum by Henry Irving. And here let me say that I confine what I say to the working of the old Lyceum; I have no knowledge whatever of the new – except that, standing on the same space, it holds in its auditorium twice as many people as could find place in the old. In Irving's time the old Lyceum held some two thousand people all told; I am advised that it now holds with convenience some four thousand – perhaps an eighth more than Drury Lane. Let me also say that in such figures as I give I trust to my notebooks and such memoranda as from time to time I made, with the expressed consent of Sir Henry Irving, for future use. At his death I handed over, of course, all the books and property of all kinds to his executors.

I take a period of twenty years from the summer of 1878 to the summer of 1898, a time of great prosperity – such a time as may not be counted upon in the permanent management of a theatre. Then, if ever, was the time when an enthusiastic and bold-hearted player could in his own person do what in other nations is done for the theatre by the State or the Municipality. For twenty years Henry Irving conducted his theatre so well and to such splendid purpose that throughout the world it was held as the exemplar of what might be done in dramatic art, and it – and he – were held in international honour. During those twenty years he played in London in all six hundred and twenty weeks, divided into some twenty seasons varying in length from thirteen to forty-seven weeks. In this time, or rather for this time, he spent in expenses of his theatre nearly a million of money – or, to be more exact, over £965,000 sterling. Expenses of the stage alone (counting in thousands of pounds only) totalled as follows:

	£
Salaries	280,000
Supers	16,000
Stage staff and expenses (expenses of manufacture not included)	100,000
Lighting (gas, electric, and limelight)	32,000
Orchestra	47,000
The cost of producing plays (without including plays bought or produced, but not included in the period)	153,000

The expenses of what is called the 'Front of the House' were as follows:	
General staff of the theatre (not including the stage)	30,000
Expenses of working	56,000
Sundries	12,000

Then there were incidental expenses difficult to place in any departmental category:	
Law and audit	3,000
Insurance	7,000
Expenditure on the upkeep of the theatre and its belongings	8,000

Other working expenses included	
Printing	13,000
Newspaper advertising	57,000
Bill-posting	15,000

In addition to the above and many other expenses were the purchase of plays, and authors' fees amounting to some £13,000 for the period.

In considering the above figures as some sort of standard of expenses of a great theatre, it must be borne in mind that the heaviest items of the lot – those of salaries and expenses of production – are, from the fact that the theatre was a private one, in reality much lower than they should be for matters of comparison. With regard to salaries, Henry Irving is only put down at a nominal salary – nominal to an actor of his 'drawing' power. It is a practical custom in England for an actor who is also a manager to put himself in the salary list at only a 'living wage' and not at his earning power. Irving thus put himself at £70 per week; so that out of the £280,000 above given only £43,000 in twenty years is charged for his services. Actors of his calibre (when there are any) get quite £100 for each performance, so that, had that computation been entered on the books of the theatre, another

£320,000 at least should have been added to the £280,000, making by this item alone in all £600,000. So also in the case of the 'twin star,' Miss Ellen Terry. Her engagement was made in such a way that for London her salary was only about one-third of what she got in the provinces, and less than a fourth of what she got in America. If her salary were to be put down at its value – comparative to her earnings when paid as salary in later years – the total would become over £750,000. In such case the weekly salary list for London computed from the figures given above, instead of being £450, as I calculated, would be over £1,200 per week. And the weekly expense account would spring from £1,400 (without counting rent rates and taxes, and authors' fees) to over £2,100.

I in no way take Irving's figures as final for a National Theatre; but only as showing what was actually paid by a capable and earnest man doing his best for the art he loved and for the good of the drama and the theatre in their highest aspects, and without any statistical aim.

But even suppose that the services of actors adequate to the class of performance could be obtained in the general working for the sums set down for the working of the old Lyceum, the cost of working the National Theatre for a year of fifty weeks (leaving two weeks for cleaning, redecorating, &c., on the average) would run to a sum of at least £75,000 per annum. Take the average receipts for each week 'by and large' at £1,000 – which would be quite as great as could be expected in a theatre working all the year round – there would be an annual deficit of at least £25,000, which would have to be met in some way. Capitalise this annual sum at the rate of Consols – 2½ per cent. –and a primary endowment of £1,000,000 sterling would be required.

At the present rate of Consols – 87¾ per cent., say 88 per cent. to leave a margin – the initial cost, £500,000, and the fund for upkeep, £1,000,000, would require an issue of 2½ per cent. Consols of some £1,700,000 sterling. Such would be the price which would have to be paid for the furnishing and upkeep – reckoned at the lowest figures – of a National Theatre. With this knowledge before them, statesmen could reckon whether that which was to be purchased would be worth the price. For their proper understanding of the subject certain matters would have to be considered – matters not of figures, but of possibility of fulfilling the duty imposed by such an undertaking. The building of the theatre and its adequate equipment would be a comparatively easy task. To these would come expert artists, workmen, and men of business, just as they do in the case of a private concern. But the making of laws and regulations for the government of the public institution, as the theatre would necessarily become after its launching, whether it were founded by the State, the city, a philanthropic syndicate, or a munificent individual, and the selection of the *personnel* of the governing body would be a seriously difficult matter. In the bye-laws careful provision would have to be made against misuse of power, nepotism, peculation, favouritism in all forms, and the thousand-and-one manifestations of personal dislikings and jealousies which are apt to hamper the steps of pure justice in artistic life. By the nature of the undertaking anyone appointed to the governing body would have to be appointed for life, or with an age limit and a pension – all of course subject to good conduct. It is of the essence of the desirability of any form of public service that it is continuous service, not subject to chance or merely commercial change. If there were not such advantage, no man whose services would be of any worth would forgo the possibilities of private enterprise and merge his personal ambitions in work of public import. In this matter public service must be regarded as a sort of insurance – the hedging against chance – a sheltering one's individual risks behind the laws of average. It is for this reason that adequate service can usually be had for public work under the standard wage of its class.

In the figures which I have given no provision is made for pensions. I do not feel bound to state any, as I am not formulating any scheme for founding a National Theatre, but only suggesting certain matters which would have to be considered in case the advisability of such an institution should be favourably considered by the powers that be. In Austria, where certain theatres are under public management, their actors belong to the Civil Service, and are under and amenable to the rules governing such. And, should our own State take up the matter of a National Theatre, there would be much clamour for a similar system.

Out of this rises another question, which would be sure to come to the fore: Would the great body of actors, theatre managers, and theatre-workers, outside the tally of those employed in the National Theatre, gain any material advantage? It is hard to imagine how they would. That private enterprises would suffer from the opposition of an endowed or subsidised theatre, not answerable to ordinary commercial conditions, would be apparent; and where an ordinary theatre suffers in pocket the suffering necessarily runs right down the line. But wherein could be an advantage? At present there are in this country many thousands of actors of one kind or another. There are, according to the *Era* Almanack, throughout the country more than six hundred licensed theatres, each of which employs a considerable number of players and workers of various kinds. This number does not include music halls, of which there are a vast number, and most of which employ a certain number of players who oscillate between the playhouse and the music hall as the pinch of poverty compels or the desire of wealth urges. The question of stage operatives will not be considered here; they have their own guilds and trade unions; we are only concerned, for the present at all events, with the players. Accepting, then, the British players as but ten thousand, only a very small percentage of any class of them could be provided for in a National Theatre. In this, however large it might be, there would only be possibilities for a hundred at most ('supers' are not considered in any way as 'actors' in stage-land). It would doubtless be good in the long run for the few who were chosen; but the many left, numbering ninety-nine per cent. of the entire body, would have to bear amongst them an evil far exceeding the others' good.

There would, doubtless, be also contingent evils: the manifest advantages to mediocre players to be settled for life by an engagement in the National Theatre would beget intriguing of the fiercest kind. A player looking for such an engagement would naturally try to rally to his service all the forces which he could influence; so that the official or body with whom finally the selection rested would have an uneasy time in the storm-centre of such opposing forces.

Again, the *personnel* of the officials would be a difficult matter were such an institution to be founded; and it would not be long before charges of favouritism or self-interest began to fly wide. *Quis custodiet ipsos custodes* would be an important apophthegm in the case of officials entrusted with such varied and irresponsible patronage. Indeed, the directorate would be difficult of choice. A director or chairman of directors for such a purpose should have a lot of almost opposing qualifications. He should have large stage knowledge and experience; he should know what is called 'the world'; he should have natural and cultivated taste; and, supremest quality of all, he should have an open mind – with the least possible share of prejudice himself, and be proof against the prejudices of others. He should not be too young, since such is to be without experience, nor too old to be unreceptive of new ideas. He should be transparently as well as actually just; and yet should be stalwart in standing by his considered and matured opinions. In fact, he should be a paragon. The most natural selection would be a theatre manager who would be willing to glide his own ambitions into the channels of his new undertaking. But such an one would in no case be fairly young – young enough to have left the needed stock of energy for theatre direction; or else he would be one who, having failed in his own ambition, was seeking calmer waters for his declining years. Ambition dies hard; in the full swing of its realisation no man is willing to forgo his quest. There is also another objection to a former manager: such men have always – rightly or wrongly – fixed ideas of policy, and they have many friends and *protégés*, to many of whom they must be under some sort of obligation, even if the same be only for good wishes and unquestioning belief. Such obligations are many-winged and many-footed, and are apt to fly or crawl into the scales of justice.

This difficulty, however, need not be here considered. There are plenty of good men – good and suitable in every way, and no one who has any experience of life doubts that when the Hour strikes the Man will appear. The three points to consider are: (1) Could the thing be done at all? (2) Would the cost be prohibitive? (3) Would it be advisable: (a) in the interests of art; (b) good for the world of the theatre; (c) profitable directly or indirectly to the great public? The second of these we may almost dismiss. This is a rich country, and whatever work makes, in the estimation of Parliament, for good can have sufficient money provided for its doing. The first may be answered in the affirmative, if qualified by acceptance of the third; anything within reason can be done if the consensus of opinion is in its favour. It is in the third point that difficulty lies. 'Your *If* is the only peacemaker; much virtue in *If*,' says Touchstone.

If a National Theatre would be advisable in the interests of art, good for the world of the theatre, and profitable to the great public, then we may regard it as a work to be some day undertaken by the State.

This, always remembering, of course, that it be deemed worth the cost. But there must be no mistake about the cost. It does not do to calculate by subsidy fixed per annum or varying as required. It must be theoretically capitalised before we can consider the matter fairly. This capital amount would be *at least* a sum of £1,500,000 sterling – £1,700,000 of money at its present value. More might be required later in case receipts did not come up to the estimated amount, whatever that might be. For it must not be forgotten that if such a theatre were to justify its name as 'National,' it should be kept open as far as possible all the year round. Thus only the dwellers in other cities of the nation might visit it during their occasional staying in the capital.

Americans as Actors

In dealing with this question, it must be understood that we treat only of North America, and of one section of it only, the United States. The other sections – Canada and Mexico – are not directly concerned in the inquiry.

Every nation has its own aptitudes for certain forms of endeavour. This is partly, if not mainly, due to race, partly to climatic conditions, partly to the other conditions on which rational as well as individual life is based – those of labour, amusement, loyalty, hopes and fears, ambitions, and the circumstances which make for more or less strenuous endeavour. With regard to the racial qualities, it is hardly necessary to understand their origins or even to seek them; it is sufficient if we accept existing facts. Were we examining the history of a nation or a race such might – would be – an imperative duty, primarily undertaken for the acceptance of the very base of true understanding. Sufficient for the present purpose it is to examine how things stand today. If we wish to understand the idiosyncrasies of American character and life sufficiently to make some kind of forecast of possibilities of the future, we must primarily have a truthful estimate of the present.

The United States of America, as it exists to-day, is a nation of specialists. This does not imply that each individual deliberately sets himself or herself to a chosen task at the beginning of life, and follows it on to the logical end. Rather does it refer to the conclusions of work and life; a sort of survival of the fittest for special endeavour, each adapting himself to special needs and following the path on which he has begun, with ever-growing ardour as new possibilities develop themselves. Herein advance depends a good deal on another racial quality which in the West has become highly developed, that of adaptability. It is not sufficient for a worker to be strenuous by nature and efficient by practical effort; developing opportunities due in part to the ordinary chances of life, all make for new powers and new applications of initial forces. To speak in metaphor: progress does not run on rails, but follows the ordinary roads created or organised as the resultant of many varying needs. The United States has been for more than a century in a condition of development which has had no equal in any other part of the world, or at any other age. A vast region, containing some three million square miles of surface, came at once into habitable possibility. It is true that on the outer edges of the North American Continent the European races had found foothold and that the centre was occupied by Indians – the descendants of Asiatic races, chiefly Chinese, who lived a nomadic life, sparsely scattered over the vast and then inhospitable area, roughly grouped in tribes of varying worth and powers, but all largely if not wholly savage. The Anglo-Saxons had settled on the Eastern seaboard and had penetrated inwards, civilising as they went. The Spaniards had settled to the east and west of the South. The French occupied the centre of the South. In the North Great Britain and France contended for supremacy. At the beginning of the era of great progress the prime need was population, and the overcrowded nationalities of Europe found outlet for their surplus population. But pioneering must begin with individuals; it was only when the Famine came to Ireland in 1846-7 that the great rush of immigrants began. But when once the current had been formed its progress became continuous. Until recently the American States became the dumping ground of all the over-peopled countries. Italy, Germany, Poland, Hungary, Russia, have continuously sent enormous numbers of emigrants, purely and primarily for purposes of finding settlement. Other nations have added to the population, but from a different cause: that of seeking work; some ending in settlement and consequent fusion, others coming as workers but not remaining permanently. For illustration the Swedes, lumberers by hereditary practice, came to the forest regions; and having once done their work as foresters made permanent settlement. On the other hand, the Chinese when coming made contracts with the shipping companies to bring back to China in due course their bodies 'alive or dead.' The penalising conditions of recent legislation have largely stopped the incursion of this race. We need take no special note in this connection of either of the coloured races, Indians or Negroes. The former were the indigenous inhabitants when the Caucasians made entry and are rapidly becoming extinct. The latter are the descendants of the slaves imported chiefly in the later years of the eighteenth century, and as they do not fuse with the white races do not enter on our consideration. The negro breeds fast, and the very existence of millions who flourish in what has come to be known as the 'Black Belt' is a terror to the statesmen of the Federated States. Mexico is largely Spanish. The population of Canada is largely the result of emigration from Scotland, though, of course, other nations have sent contingents also; notably Japan in later years. Contingents of all races are now to be found within the United States.

The ultimate fusion of these many races must create what will be practically a new type. But such is as yet far off; so we need only glance at it as a possibility, and confine ourselves to things as they are. How each of the various races named will supplement each other is an ethnological problem. In race-fusion the lower as well as the higher races have beneficent part, adding physical strength, endurance, fecundity, though they may lack moral and intellectual strength. But, after all, progress does not proceed on a grade of continuous or eternal

proportions. There are set-backs as well as sudden propulsions forward; the utmost that can be expected is a *tendency* of advance.

Where American race-problems are involved it is to the United
States that we must look. Canada and Mexico are fairly constant in
their racial developments – Scotch blood in the one case and Spanish
in the other being the paramount foreign elements; but 'foreigners,'
being merged in the mass of population, must be accepted to-day as
part of the indigenous stock. And, therefore, in following the subject
before us, we must almost of necessity confine ourselves to the United
States.

Now, as the various nationalities carry with them not only their
national as well as their racial characteristics, but the customs and
habits of the places which they have left, and which may fairly be
accepted as logical developments of their predominating characteristics, we have to realise that the immigration, through a reasonable
space of years, is no negligible quantity in determining the possibilities of advance in any given direction of the nation as it exists.

Take the characteristics of these nationalities in their own habitats
and we can get a suggestion of their influence in an expanding nation.
Such influence must, of necessity, be at first of the minimum, for the
proportion of foreigners is small; but the newcomers, as expansive off-
shoots, must have their share of dispositions, customs and habits. The
German is philosophic, reasonable, industrious, calm. The Italian –
type of the Latin in our present connection – is passionate, effusive,
quick, eager, reckless, impulsive, largely swayed by emotion. These
two races, German and Latin, typify broadly the essential qualities
required within the range of the present discussion. The Irish element
we need hardly consider separately when we come to the union or
cleavage between aptitude and habit, since it resembles the Latin
rather than the German temperament. We have further, in examining
into artistic possibilities, to consider what special as well as what general elements we have to deal with.

The Latin, being demonstrative, is in the habit of displaying emotion – and in lesser degree thought and intention – by gesture. The
German, on the other hand, has a phlegm which negatives such
momentary trivialities. Any traveller knows how much easier it is to
understand – when he does not know the language – what is going on
between other persons in Southern than in Northern Europe. Take, for
instance, a shop or public vehicle – any place where prices have to be
asked and payments made. In the one case gesticulation at every
moment supplements, duplicates, or interprets speech. The quick
action of hand and finger is simply arithmetic in action: the facial
expression is as illuminative as carefully chosen words; and so on
through the whole scheme of the expression of thought. But in the
places where calmness, if not self-restraint, is usual, there is no such

help. The customary meaning of words is of paramount force; and one who does not understand the language is simply helpless. Thus the racial habit of gesticulation, or of duplicate means of expressing thought, becomes a prime quality of power or facility in the art of the stage. Of course, the practical difficulty in estimating the comparative values of racial additions to the population is that of education. Emigrants are, as a rule, not well educated. As a matter of fact they come mainly from quite the lower and poorer classes. The exception is in the case of a great number of German emigrants. In Germany every one is educated up to a certain degree, to the result that when any of them emigrate they are not immediately inferior to their surroundings, as is too often the case. Thus, broadly speaking, the German brings to the racial fusion a philosophic calm, the Latin and the Celt emotional temperament. In the last Census, 1900, the foreign born population was as follows, counting in thousands only:–

English	843,000
Scotch	234,000
Irish	1,619,000
French	104,000
Italian	484,000
Polish	170,000
Hungarian	145,000
Russian	424,000
German	2,669,000

This does not take into account the census of descendants of 'foreigners' settled in the United States. So that, as at present existing, what we may call the 'impulsive races' – French, Italian, Irish, Hungarian, Polish, number about two and a half millions; whilst the more phlegmatic races, English, Scotch, German and Russian, number four millions. As the population of the States and territories at the last census numbered (exclusive of 'Indians not taxed') some seventy-six millions, the proportion of 'foreign born' element is in no case an alarming one regarding ultimate disposition of races. It is the American custom to count as (United States) Americans all born in their own land; an exact enough custom for practical purposes, as the fusion of races becomes permanent and incoming foreigners become absolutely merged in the existing race. It is thus the existing population to which we must look for development in the emotional arts. Any variation which may come from the 'foreign' element must, as shown by the above figures, be rather on the phlegmatic than the emotional side. Let us therefore consider the question as one dependent almost entirely on existing population and local conditions.

If the number of theatres is any indication of the wishes of a people in that direction, the United States stands very well for histrionic effort. Mr. Julius Cahn gives in his compendious Theatrical Guide the names of more than two thousand six hundred theatres of varying importance in the United States, which would allow of one theatre for every 24,000 inhabitants. This compares favourably with our British average, for by the lists given in the *Era* Almanack the British theatres and music-halls total about 800, which would give an average of just about twice as many persons to each theatre.

Were our examination as to the popularity of the theatre the incidence would be altogether on the American side; but as it is relating to the native capacity for acting, it rather tends the opposite way. For even with such an evident demand for actors the indigenous supply is insufficient; there is a ready market in the United States for the services of competent players – provided, of course, that they can speak the language.

The conclusions of the statistics given are borne out by experience, which is, after all, the only convincing way of arriving at conclusions in such a matter as this, dependent largely on ever-varying factors of fallible humanity. Between the years 1883 and 1904 I spent altogether with Henry Irving in America more than four years occupied with eight theatrical tours, during which we visited every great town in the United States, North, South, East and West; so that there was plenty of opportunity of studying the trend of theatrical affairs in that great nation. Of course, as Irving travelled with his own company there was not much opportunity of comparison from within between native and imported histrionic talent. But now and again our forces, both histrionic and executive, were reinforced by local aid; and through this means, as well as by seeing the other plays given in cities and towns where we played, one came in time to have a properly-founded estimate of American suitability for the exercise of the actor's craft. Let me say here that to my mind the American workman has, as a workman, no superior. By 'workman' I mean men or women working at any craft requiring intelligence as well as labour. The statement applies to all crafts, whether or not included in the category of fine arts. We have had at times the assistance of workmen of all nationalities, but I am bound to say that the Americans were the readiest, the most capable, the steadiest, the hardest working, the most intelligent. Put an American workman opposite a new situation or a state of things with which he has had no previous experience, and he will proceed to a quicker and better result than will any other of equal experience. If he is independent to a measure not usual in older communities, what of that? A good workman should know that he is a good workman; it is part of the measure of his self-respect; and self-respect is one of the most important factors of human advance. So much for the executive workmen of the theatre; as to the actors, we only employed those of minor importance – chorus, supers, and an occasional 'young man' or 'extra lady.' On one occasion we took a whole chorus from New York and travelled them with us for the tour; and we generally supplemented the local orchestra not only with members of our own orchestra, who formed a section of the touring party, but with local extraneous performers. On one occasion we had, by the way, as one of our limelight operators, an Indian actor, who, being anxious to have experience in an intimate way of a higher stage work than his own, took that opportunity of study. In Boston we nearly always had supers who were students of Harvard, and on several occasions, in various places, an enterprising reporter undertook, *incognito*, that humble service for the purpose of more intimate observation.

But it is from the auditorium, not the stage, that the true merit of actors must in the long run be judged. Their art is an art of result, and if they do not achieve that satisfactorily they are not successful in their aims, and consequently of no account. How they achieve result is not known to the audience and not cared for by them. Such is a part of the education and practice of their craft or 'mystery.' And although it may be of academic importance to thoughtful students of work in general, it cannot be of much importance to the public, who only care for completed work which will please, amuse, or interest them.

It is here that we arrive at the supreme quality of American endeavour; and in an art which depends for great success on individual qualities or gifts, it is of added value. The American actor knows how to make the most of his powers and opportunities. To this end he studies and practises endlessly. In a word, he looks to his equipment for his work and strives to be well-educated in it; and here he falls into line with the other strivers of his nation. It is this which makes America a nation of experts. One and all, its people strive for complete mastery over some subject. There is nothing too small to undertake in all seriousness; to which to bring the whole of one's thought and energy and skill. Look at the result. In a thousand small industries America is easily ahead in the race for wealth, and in special articles supplies the world. The catch of a door, a towel rail, a sponge bag, the case of an eye-glass, a penholder, a lemon squeezer, 'squeezer' playing cards – all these and myriad others attest American inventiveness and application. The geniuses who made wooden nutmegs by the ton and turned out whole ship-loads of manufactured oats were, though fraudulent and immoral to the last degree, in a sense national benefactors, for they showed in a practical way that *nothing* in the commercial world is beneath consideration. I have known a great fortune made by manufacturing ordinary luggage labels. But then the tag was the best of its kind and sold at a price which forbade competition. Again, I have known a simple paper bag as the machinery for the accretion of great wealth. Look at the success of the Yale lock, the Dennison tag, the tram line, the concentrated cattle whose exploitation adorns our dead walls, and a hundred similar possibilities.

The same racial spirit which looks at possibilities with either the telescope or the microscope guides the stage. The grouping of theatrical management shows the telescopic aspect; the vigorous and careful way in which the daring aspirant to the third row of the chorus equips herself for other fields of conquest makes the microscopic aspect. Indeed, one who wished to put the question into an apophthegm might to-day parallel Thackeray's witty saying: 'The staple products of Ireland are whiskey and manslaughter,' and declare that as seen largely by European eyes, 'the staple products of America are toilet paper and countesses.'

For my own part, I have now for some years held that the great impulse towards theatrical life will come from Americans when acting is accepted in that country as an available industry. It is right to say that at present there is no bar to its acceptance. There is not the same violent opposition in that country to those who make the choice of stage life that holds more or less in all the European nations. Of course, the situation is always looked in the face by parents and guardians, and the pros and cons summed up and weighed. No doubt the present difficulties are at times paramount and the ultimate outlook is dreaded; but the difficulty thus regarded is tentative rather than perpetual. The more and the quicker that young people, not as yet belonging to stage life, join the ranks of the actors, the easier it will be for those who follow them, and the lesser the strain of anxiety on the part of relatives. For with growing numbers of a class whose education has tended to conventionality rather than to unconventionality there is greater social security. In fact, to use an analogy, a new atmosphere is created. The world of the stage is like all other worlds in the incidence of cosmic laws; and as size is a necessary condition for the creation of an atmosphere in astronomical creation, so in the lesser world the law holds. Thus we must look before long for a great American accretion – somewhat in proportion to the vastness of the population – to the ranks of stage workers.

At present, so far as I have seen through the experience of more than a quarter of a century in the working of a great theatre, the American recruits are admirable workers. We had experience of a fair number of them in the Lyceum, and they all seemed to do well and 'get on' quickly. This was largely due to their own exertions. They always studied, not only the subject of their immediate work, but the things at which they are aiming. The stage, as a whole, is a world of perpetual advance, but as the mechanism is entirely individual its general powers are limited by the capacity of the players. I use the word 'capacity' not in its common meaning of power of assimilation, intellectual or physical; but as conveying an idea of existing power whether natural or acquired. And therefore, as the players enlarge their ideas, so the stage advances. It takes a long training to make an actor. There are few accepted laws which can guide or rule; it is only by acquired experience that the actor can act that almost unconscious familiarity with his work which will supply or take the place of principles of art. One might as well expect to be an expert stenographer by knowing by heart a manual of shorthand, as to be an actor without having acted. The whole thing is in the doing. The training and equipment are of course antecedent; and it is in this preparatory stage of art work that application and its result – education – are of value. Actors should always bear in mind that success in a part is not the reward of a spasmodic effort, but of the long, slow, patient, strenuous attempts at perfection. Shakespeare's wise saying: 'The scholar's melancholy, which is emulation,' is hard to understand outside the arts. But there it is altogether understandable; there it belongs. In the emulation necessary for perfection – even for its seeking – the whole world is open: and amongst the contestants is one's own self. To use a phrase in the terminology of athleticism: in the breathing of records one's own record may be included. This is the prime quality of advance, the active principle of self-sacrificing effort. And I am bound to say that I have always noticed it in American actors. The danger which attends it is, that ambitious youth may take the striving for fitness to succeed as the striving necessary for success in an immediate object. Strenuousness is much in the art world; but it is not all. This reminds one of the story of the determined Scot, who declared that he would become a *maestro* of the violin. When his friends expressed doubt as to his powers, and asked on what quality he relied for success, he answered:–

'A'll do it by main strength!'

The American has great self-reliance as well as much strength of purpose, and if the winning of success is to be achieved by application he will doubtless win it. But he, like all others, must remember that art is a world by itself, and has, in addition to the laws which govern all other human efforts, its own laws, which must be observed under penalty of failure. In that world matters cannot be 'rushed.' *Ars longa* has come to be accepted as a truism unneeding explanation. The very strenuous quality in its people which makes America great stands in their road in the doing of art work. Strenuousness has its own self-consciousness, and self-consciousness is the bane of true art. Theoretically we might argue that the result of this very strenuousness as applied in wrong direction would lead to failure; thus the quality which makes good artisans would make bad artists. And this is exactly what happens in fact. Stage art is an excellent opportunity of testing the theory, for here so much depends on the individuality of the artist that the general drift of things is only a minor cause of happenings. We find that American players are admirable in the smaller parts, but that in the higher walks the same relative excellence is not observed. In all arts there are many levels between excellence and greatness; in stage art, with again varieties of individuality as a cause, the levels are endless. In organising a theatrical company a manager could hardly do better than to recruit a full share of American players; but in all probability he would have to look in the theatre world generally for his 'stars.' Of course, it must be here borne in mind that every nation has its own social observances, its own peculiarities of accent, its own types of character; and that for the reproduction of these certain education or experience is necessary. So that if reproduction of national type, or manner, or accent is required, the best results can be had from those artists who are familiar with them. It used to be supposed that a fully equipped player should be able to assume at will accents and such like accessories of character; but a too rigid adherence to this belief is throwing away natural advantages. Surely a 'Down-east,' or an 'Out-west' type can be better assumed by one who knows the special world represented. On the other hand, the personal peculiarities – whether they be due to race or nationality – which enable actors to represent, almost without study, certain strongly marked characters, are out of place in the representation of classical characters, who on the stage represent average or natural types of emotion or passion. The perfect Hamlet, for instance, or perfect Ophelia should not have a brogue, or a twang, or a lisp, or even that Attic broadness which can win fame and fortune on the variety stage. A Romeo and Juliet who chewed, the one tobacco and the other gum, would be out of place even in a canvas Verona. On the other hand, it would be fatal for Hamlet or Macbeth, Juliet or Beatrice, to be self-conscious in the midst of a scene of sweeping passion. Self-consciousness and strenuousness are most excellent qualities – when in their proper places. And their proper place is in the educational stage of advance – in the preparation for supreme effort, not during the effort itself.

Dead-heads

The term 'dead-head' in its colloquial sense has come to us from America in recent years. It may be interesting to examine how it came and its exact meaning. To this end it will be well to clear the ground by getting rid of special meanings so as to leave only one issue.

In Wright's English *Dialect Dictionary* two meanings of the word are given:

'(a) A bottle of wine, or spirits, that has been emptied.

(b) A member of a football or cricket team called upon to play at a pinch.'

The *Century Dictionary* gives another:

'In founding: The extra length of metal given to cast gun. It serves to receive the dross, which rises to the surface of the liquid metal, and would be, were it not for the dead-head, at the muzzle of the gun.

Again, in the *New English Dictionary* (Murray) another meaning of a nautical kind is given, as a fixed post on a quay to which hawsers may he made fast.

Another authority gives the word:

'In Florida, a log so soaked with water that it will not float. Opposite term is *live log*.' – *Dictionary of Americanisms*. Sylvan Clapin. (Weiss and Co., New York, n.d.)

We come finally to the accepted meaning of the word as in use at the present time. It came into the language, as did a good many other words, via slang, which the *Pall Mall Gazette* in its very early days dubbed 'new language.' It may therefore he taken to have originally a special rather than a general meaning; but what that special meaning was it is a little difficult to understand, as may be seen from the following quotations as given by various authorities:

'One who receives free tickets for theatres, public conveyances, &c.' (Colloq., U.S.). *Webster's Dictionary*. (Bell, 1897)

'One who rides in a public conveyance, visits the theatre, or obtains anything of value, without payment (United States).' – *Imperial Dictionary*. Ogilvie. (Blackie's, 1882)

'Colloq. (orig. U.S.) a person admitted without payment to a theatre performance, a public conveyance, &c.' – Murray's *New English Dictionary*. (Clarendon Press, 1897)

'(U.S.) one who is allowed, without payment, to ride in a public carriage, sit in a theatre, or hold a privilege having a money value.' – *Twentieth Century Dictionary*. (Chambers, 1905)

'(Cf., 0. Dan. död thoved, a fool), one who is allowed to ride in a public conveyance, to attend a theatre or other place of entertainment, or to obtain any privilege having its public price without payment (U.S.).' – *Century Dictionary*. (Century Company, New York, copyright, 1889)

'(U.S.) One who receives gratis any service or accommodation for which the general public is expected to pay; as dead-heads on a train, or in a theatre.' – *Standard Dictionary*. (Funk and Wagenels, New York, 1901)

So far the term seems to apply only to those who travel or get amusement free – an enlargement which would in itself show its American origin, for in England the word is not usually applied to free travel. The authorities of slang give more varied meanings, all of which have 'internal evidence' – to use Whately's phrase – of transatlantic origin:

'One who stands about the bar to drink at the expense of others.' – (*Dictionary of Slang, Jargon, and Cant*. Albert Barrere and Charles G. Leland. (Bell, London, 1897)

'Dead-head (dead-beat or dead-hand) one who obtains something of commercial value without special payment or charge; spec. a person who travels by rail, visits theatres, &c., by means of free passes. Also verb (American).' – *Dictionary of Slang and Colloquial English*. John S. Farmer and W. E. Henley. (Routledge, London, 1905)

Farmer and Henley quote De Vere's *Americanisms*, 'one who lives at the hotel without charge.' They quote also from the London *Daily Telegraph* of 1888 in criticising a certain opera 'stale enough to warrant the most confirmed dead-head in declining to help make a house.' A confirmation of the origin of the word is, by the way, conveyed in the peculiarly American wording, 'to help make.' We shall see, later on in this article, the utility of this quotation.

'Persons who drink at a bar, ride in an omnibus or railroad car, travel in steamboat, or visit the theatre without charge, we called *dead-heads*. These consist of the engineers, conductors, and labourers on railroads; the keepers of hotels; the editors of newspapers.' – *Dictionary of Americanisms*. John Russell Bartlett. (Little, Brown and Co., Boston, U.S., 1877)

It is worthy of note that the word is not in *Johnson's Dictionary* either of 1799 or in the editions of 1827, 1865, or 1871 (edited by Latham); nor is it in *Wedgwood's Etymological Dictionary* (Trubner, 1888) or in *Skeat's Etymological Dictionary* (Oxford Press, 1898). From which, in conjunction with the extracts given above, it may be taken for granted that the word was not in general use in Britain till towards the end of the nineteenth century.

In all the authorities the theatre forms an important part in the definition. This is as it should be, for the word is manifestly of theatrical origin. It would be little less than absurd to try to find in it merely an enlargement of the term as used in nautical matters, gun-founding,

Florida lumber-work, cricket or football matches, or in the baser pleasures of the table or the drinking-bar. The old Danish of the *Century Dictionary* does not apply at all; whatever also he may be, the dead-head, as such, is certainly not a fool, though the term might possibly he correctly applied to 'other party' of his transactions.

If the origin of the word be examined, the world of the theatre is the only one which can supply a logical cause. Up to the time when mechanical aids to checking of theatrical account were invented or adapted, the only cheek which a manager had was to 'count the house' as it is called, a simple process – exactly what its name implies. Those parts of the house for which special tickets were issued, showing the exact seat purchased, were easy to cheek. There were not so many of them and there was so speedy and simple a method of identification that any fraud attempted by the attendants was a dangerous undertaking. The parts of the theatre open to possibilities of fraud were those to which the public paid admission as they came in. They came in a rush; and it is at such times that dishonesty has its chance. And so collusion between the seller of the ticket and the receiver of it used to be sadly common. It therefore became at least advisable for any manager who suspected fraud to go or send someone to the pit or gallery – the unbooked seats – during the course of the evening to count the people. The money-takers (sellers of admission tickets) and check-takers were responsible for the entry of the numbers thus returned. The money-taker's return should show all who paid, so that the total number, less free admissions, should be represented by cash. On this basis, which was a factor in each night's work, anyone who did not represent money was considered 'dead' i.e., *non est*. Now, to count a large crowd of people is no easy task, but one requiring certain skill and experience. The easiest way, and that alone with any chance of success, is when they are all seated. It then becomes possible, by standing a little in front at the side, to number them with fair accuracy. Only the heads are visible and so the count becomes one of 'heads.' And thus also the 'dead' visitors are dead-heads. It is all perfectly simple and logical; and there is no other means of arriving at the origin of the word which would or could become acceptable. The application of the term outside theatres – for instance, to travel – is due entirely to the intellectual superiority of the American criminal over his British brother. With his better education and more adaptable nature, the American workman in this field of labour has invented new ways of achieving the success at which he aims.

So much for the origin of the word. Its meaning, developed on the slang side, is altogether a matter of the local standard of morals. In its inception the existence or aptitude of the dead-head is not wrong – has nothing to do with any standard of ethics; it is simply a fact. And the question of fact must be established before the question of ethics can arise. If, therefore, we take dead-heads as a body, we must first differentiate them before we condemn. This, in both accuracy and justice, is necessary, for the term as commonly used is, as may be inferred, one of reproach. The dead-head who boasts of his segregation as such is but a poor creature, and may well be classed in the great scheme of utility with the empty bottle, the water-soaked log, the superfluous gun-metal, the insensate post on the quay – though, indeed, this latter has a value, albeit a passive one. In fact, the further investigation must be based on the proposition that though the dead-head is the exerciser of a free franchise, the exerciser of a free franchise is not of necessity a dead-head in the ethical sense of the word. Confining ourselves for the moment to the theatre, let us examine the exceptions which make the basic proposition clear; we can afterwards, if we will, apply the reasoning to phases of life other than the theatre.

In the management of a theatre there are so many varying conditions – so many persons have to be brought together, so many different interests are involved, so many things have to be remembered in connection with the carrying out of the high policy of the endeavour – that mere money value ceases to represent either the aim of the undertakers or the means of achieving it. As in the great scheme of one life or a nation, immediate and tangible reward is not the only thing desirable. Money is, truly enough, an important factor in the winning of success, and a demonstrable proof of successful effort; but it is not all. Continuity within possible bounds has to be achieved; so that good result in the present becomes largely a further investment of capital. A theatre in these days has to be kept open for at least some forty to forty-five weeks in the year. Each city has its own 'catchment area.' and the supply of theatregoers is by such limited in greater or lesser degree. Take, for instance, London as an example – the greatest and perhaps the most difficult on account of the enormous actual proportions and varying percentages of its fluctuating population.

In round numbers the inhabitants of London of all classes within the police district, and including the City, number some six and a half millions. In addition there is an influx on each day of perhaps twenty thousand visitors – visitors, nearly all of whom, as strangers coming to enjoy themselves, visit the theatres, as they do other places of recreation. The stay of each of such persons may be short or long; but take it that they stay on an average a week, and that during that week they go (such of them as go at all) a couple of times.

Thus we have two forms of population, resident and transient, which have to be considered separately, as they are under such different conditions. Let us take the resident population first. The six and a half millions resident in the police districts may fairly represent in family life groups of five – father, mother, and three children. This is a little larger than the average for the nation. The statistics of 1901 show the family average to be in England, Wales, and Scotland 4.62, and in Ireland 4.90. Of the family of five let us take it that (if they are theatre-goers at all) two of them now and again enjoy the play. Say that if only half of them be playgoers (it is a very small average for the poorer class, who are the larger class, as the theatre is practically their only indoor amusement, and prices in theatres are regulated to suit all pockets), we get out of the residents a body of some one million three hundred thousand playgoers. Take it that these go on an average eight times in a year. (This, class by class, is a small average – much less than reality.) So that all told, out of the resident population, we may expect – allowing nearly half a million for accidents, sickness, or other causes – ten million attendances per annum.

Of the transient population a larger average of attendances should be expected, since they largely come to enjoy – and, at any rate, do enjoy – whatever may bring them. If for each day twenty thousand visitors – a number fixed long ago, and not for this purpose – represents the influx, and if we take them arriving on only five days out of the seven, we get an influx of one hundred thousand per week. Such visitors remain varying periods; but, to get a base somewhere, let us take it that on an average they remain for a week each. This class mainly consists of individuals, or married folks coming in pairs and not family groups of five, so that the family average does not apply. Let us also surmise that out of the one hundred thousand one-half do not go to the theatre at all; thus we should get a weekly influx of theatregoers of some fifty thousand. Each of these would see at least two plays (again a small average, as London is the home of theatrical production and the place of greatest completeness in the art), so that we get one hundred thousand theatregoers each week, or five million per annum from the visitors.

Thus we tap a total of some fifteen million persons at least who attend a performance.

In London there are some fifty-eight theatres. So that if we take them as performing six times a week with a fair percentage of matinées in addition, we get in round numbers some four hundred theatre performances each week in London, or, in a season of fifty weeks, twenty thousand performances.

With twenty thousand performances and fifteen million attendances we get on a rough average an audience of some seven hundred and fifty paying persons in each theatre at each performance. Experience shows that these figures are fairly correct. It is, of course, impossible to obtain with accuracy such figures. Theatres differ in size and plays in 'drawing' quality, so that the laws of average cannot be anywhere applied. But it is a primary condition of theatre management that the house must be large enough to meet occasional strain. It is by this means only that a working average of receipts can be obtained; and without this the exchequer of the theatre cannot be computed or even exist.

Thus only a small measure of common sense is required to understand that in the long run in each theatre there are seats which will not be occupied by the paying public, and are, therefore, without added cost, available for managerial use.

It is here that we find the actual working possibility of the dead-head system.

Here it is also where the dead-head question bifurcates.

We have already seen that there are dead-heads *de facto* who are not ethically or morally culprits in the matter. These are those who, though they do not represent money in the house, do stand for something else. Those not learned in the policy and the difficulties of theatrical management can have no idea of either the size or importance of this class. A brief survey, and an analysis of the component elements, may bring enlightenment.

Here it is that this class in its turn again bifurcates – and we get two great divisions: those who are guests pure and simple, and those who are guests with a reason, i.e., one based on service of some form, not usually payable in cash. Let us take them in order – the guests first.

Even here there are classes, mainly two – guests from personal cause, and what may be called 'official' guests. In the former are the family, relations, and friends of the manager, and of some of his most important officials before and behind the curtain. To this class may he added such free admissions as are given to the families of those employed in the theatre who do not give *quid pro quo* in any direct form, but whose loyalty is thus secured or upheld. These comprise the authors, the actors, the composers, scene-painters, 'producers' of various kinds, costumiers, property-makers, perruquiers. These in themselves compose a numerous body. Much of their work is special, so that, although only a few take part in the preparations of any individual play, there are many of each kind who occasionally aid; and such, of course, have to be included in the 'courtesy' list of the theatre. Most artists of one kind or another are specialists in national customs or historical periods, and, as expert knowledge is largely required, the list is always being added to. By a very natural process this courtesy list is extended largely to those engaged in other similar enterprises. Theatre managers are hospitable in practice as well as in intent, and to the personnel of other theatres are extended habitually facilities of enjoyment or study. The art world generally is a big world, though a world of its own, and the camaraderie of art is at once brotherly and comprehensive. This is as it should be in a world of creative art. The 'outsider' of to-day may he the 'insider' of to-morrow or a later day. And when he comes to work for a particular theatre it is well that his education should be as effective as possible. Though to the audience playgoing is a pleasure – though such may not be altogether the purpose of the drama – to those engaged in it it is an education. An artist perfects himself by practice, and practice can only rise to its best when working on data of a well-stored mind. Moreover, as mechanical possibilities enlarge with scientific advance, it is necessary that stage producers and actors should keep abreast of the advance of their craft. It is very seldom indeed that the audience of a London theatre does not contain its percentage of this class. They are in no sense dead-heads in the popular meaning of the word, though, of course, they are in the original or technical meaning. They are guests, and welcome guests too – this invariably in a well-conducted play-house. They do not come as a rule 'on sight,' though special individuals have at times this privilege. They come either by request or on request.

The class of 'official' guests mainly comprises persons who have either a community of interest with the theatre or the play, or whose general work is or may be of ultimate benefit to either of them. Such, for instance, are newspaper critics doing their work, certain journalists not doing for the occasion special theatrical work, but who belong to the cult of theatrical criticism or who write from time to time useful paragraphs; authors who write for or about the play; some workers who belong to the higher offices of railway service or transport of other kinds, who work in conjunction with theatre officials, and who have therefore many opportunities of making themselves useful or agreeable; printers who do theatre work – posters, playbills, programmes, streamers, lithos, throw-aways, or any of the many forms of theatre advertising; managers of bill-posting establishments or companies; tradesmen who lend for stage purposes furniture, carpets, *bric-à-brac*, or any matters used as properties; florists, who beautify entrances, stairways, and passages by means of their special art; and picture dealers and print publishers, who lend their goods and chattels for the decoration of the various walls. The above are in no sense – except that of being included in the checking of the receipts of the house – dead-heads. They simply pay in a different way, that is all – in service or 'in meal or malt' in some form.

There is another order of 'official' guests who are, though in accountancy dead-heads, yet give *quid pro quo*. These are the holders of what we called 'bill orders.' In the practical working of a theatre the privileges given to them are rather in the category of 'rights' than of benefactions. One of the most important departments of a theatre is that of publicity. It is necessary that the public should be well informed of what is going on; and to this end many devices (many of there commonplace and usual, others special and opportunist) are resorted to. To the first of these divisions belong advertisements in newspapers in various traditional forms – 'leader' page, 'outer sheet,' or in some other particular part of the broadsheet mutually arranged and always adhered to. As a rule these columns are amongst the most productive of the advertising pages or columns. In former days – up to some forty or fifty years ago, and in the provincial cities and towns much later – theatre managers did not pay for their advertisements at all in cash, but gave to the newspapers an organised privilege, that of issuing on their own account orders for certain seats in various parts of the house, which were reserved for them either for every night or at certain performances. The way that the newspaper proprietor recouped himself was this: he would – except when he wanted to use the seats himself or for his family or friends – give the orders, generally printed for parties of two, to his advertisement canvassers, who would in turn give them to persons who gave advertisements or arranged them as an inducement to patronise that particular paper. Before the time of that custom the newspaper reporters used to have, for purposes of 'news,' to bribe the hall-keeper of the theatre to give them early copies of the playbill announcing the coming 'attractions.' Both these customs have, except in a few places, been long ago superseded.

The other general method of publicity is by bill-posting, i.e., displaying on walls the bills of announcement which are printed in as interesting or as showy forms of attractiveness as is possible. This department of work in organised shape began with theatres, but was found so advantages by other trades that now, and for many years past, the theatrical work is only a fraction of the mass. Bill-posting is a comparatively expensive process, especially as it appeals almost entirely to the 'patrons' of the lower-priced seats. Almost by universal custom the rent paid for such posting on walls or hoardings erected for the purpose is one penny per week per sheet 'double crown,' 'royal,' or other size and shape as may be arranged. Bills for posting are very carefully arranged and designed, and certain men have made fortunes of greater or lesser degree in printing or posting them. As these bills run to various sizes, one sheet or many – each bill, when completed, being a separate entity, no matter how many sheets go to make it up – the rental price of a single bill can be easily estimated. Bills run to four, six, ten, twelve, and so on up to as much as fifty, sixty, or a hundred sheets. Very large bills, by the way, are necessarily limited in number, as there are not many 'stands' (as they are called) where they can be posted. These bills vary in shape – 'streamers' for instance, are usually long and of the biggest letters that can be provided by the printing trade. In this category are 'picture paper' – so-called lithographs – which term has been adopted as a generic one in the printing trade. Some of these 'lithos' are so large that they have to be printed from great wooden blocks (stones of sufficient size not being obtainable), generally of pear-wood, especially put together for the purpose. The doing of all this work, printing and posting, has been specialised by the needs and size of the work itself.

But in addition to these forms of bills and the posting of them are others which have special use. Keepers of small shops, generally in unimportant thoroughfares, like to make their windows attractive or to put boards on or outside their premises to the same effect. To this end smaller bills are printed, which are usually known as 'window bills' in sizes of 'double crown' or 'folio.' Those who so place theatre bills are paid for so doing not in cash but in kind.

Special 'bill orders' are provided by the management, which are supposed to be given to such exhibitors of bills, one for two persons for the pit or gallery each week. In practice this is made an average matter, the cards being sent 'when business allows,' which is naturally when the first rush of the new play or new production is over. There are some few persons whose window display is of such importance that seats for the better part of the house, dress circle, or even stalls, are sent. These are usually the proprietors of popular 'hotels' in leading streets or in suburbs. There are very few of such places, and they are very select in their displays. It used formerly to be the custom to give the bill orders through the 'bill inspectors,' who supplied them to the various exhibitors. But experience having shown that some of them – for they were a very human class – were too often paid in malt rather than meal for their service in selecting recipients of the privilege, we made a new method in the old Lyceum Theatre some thirty years ago. We issued the bill orders direct from the management. Careful lists were kept of those entitled to receive them, and the letters were duly posted. This stopped, so far as it could be stopped, the gathering of such privilege tickets into unscrupulous hands, where they could be utilised as marketable commodity. In America, where admission prices are much larger than in Britain, the bill-order system used to be a heavy tax on visiting companies. In contracts between local theatres and travelling companies it is usual for the theatres to provide 'locals,' in which are included the posting of bills, it being the duty of the travelling 'show' to provide so much 'paper' in designated forms. Now and again a wily manager, instead of paying rent for his posting, would pay in bill orders, so that on certain nights quite a large number of admissions which were 'dead-head' in the travellers' accountancy would be amongst the checks to be counted. When seats fetching one to three dollars (four shillings to twelve shillings) were so occupied this was a heavy drain or 'hold-off' from the weekly receipts. Some of us, who took very large percentages of the total receipts, found that where this system was in vogue it was cheaper to pay for the posting ourselves – or, what was better, to do without any such posting at all. I have known, before such matters wore looked into and arranged for the future, the bill orders for a week's visit to run into a couple of hundred pounds. The hardship of it was that it was the big stars only who suffered, for every holder of a bill order was sure to turn up at their performances; whilst in the case of lesser lights, when there was plenty of room, they would never come at all. In many ways the system of bill orders was imperfect and led to numerous abuses. It was on an entirely wrong base, and has no place at all in a less crude and better ordered state of affairs.

Certain admissions have to be arranged for, which are 'official' in another way. Amongst these are Lord Chamberlain and police – 'arranged for' because it is of the essence of security that a check-taker is not empowered to admit anybody of any kind or in any circumstances without placing a voucher for such admission in his check box. The police claim the right that the policeman on duty and wearing his service badge shall be admitted to theatres, not to stay and enjoy, but to make his inspections, and so forth. It is a privilege which no sensible man does or can object to. The presence or occasional visit of such officers is not only in itself a protection to both management and audience, but is an overt proof of security – a valuable aid to an enjoyment of a kind that requires intellectual abstraction. The Lord Chamberlain, who is responsible under the Theatres Act of 1843 for the licensing of all theatres, as distinguished from music-halls, has a similar power. But it is very sparingly used, and always in the most courteous and thoughtful way.

The above classes of unpaying visitors to theatres, of course, all belong to the dead-head class in its accountancy sense, but do not come into the meaning of the word as the public of to-day understand it. They come into the dictionary meaning simply in the sense that they do not pay in the same way as the rest of the public, but the cause of their coming does not touch on ethics. In reality they are 'guests' or 'workers' rather than dead-heads, especially in the slang meaning of the latter.

Before we get to the dead-head in the base aspect – one who has no claim to ask for admission, and whose only ground for asking is that he is mean in spirit – there are two other classes to be considered. These may be really classed as one, inasmuch as they are present because the management asks them for its own purpose. The first is not a welcome guest, neither is he an overt worker; this is what the French call the *claque*, a class happily rare in this country, but who, to my own knowledge, have in former days existed, though whether they are still to the fore I do not know. Their *rationale* can be best explained from their existence in Paris and elsewhere on the Continent. In certain French theatres and opera-houses there is a sort of official or, rather, a hanger-on, who draws salary and expenses. This is the *chef du claque*, whose business it is to provide a staff, who applaud as directed. At the outset such an arrangement seems to be entirely wrong, but I have heard it defended with a certain show of reason. The public, who are, in the main, most kindly disposed, do not always understand artistic values, and are, we are told, glad to get some lead as to when to applaud. This ensures a certain appearance of approval, for the 'house' always follows suit. Moreover, the applause helps the artists in their work; it is difficult to maintain a high level of vocal or declamatory or passionate effort to an unresponsive audience. A hundred years ago, the tragedian, George Frederick Cook, dropping his assumed part for a moment, came down on one occasion to the footlights and addressed a torpid audience thus: 'Ladies and gentlemen, if you don't applaud, I can't act.'

Those foreign artists who are accustomed to the *claque* often give on their own account *douceurs* to the *chef de claque* and his merry men. Doubtless at times base use is made of such a power, and the *claque* is bribed to condemn a rival. But, of course, should such a thing be done, care would be taken to keep it secret. Certain foreign companies, when coming to this country, either bring with them their own *chef du claque* or arrange for some local individual to perform the service. I have myself in past years often seen an individual of what English people call 'foreign' appearance who seemed night after night to fulfil the function. He used to sit in one of the top boxes next to the proscenium – a position from which one can be seen from all parts of the house. He wore white gloves – very white when contrasted with the rest of his appearance – and as he always put his large hands out of the box to applaud, there was no mistaking his effort. The detonation of his hand-claps were always followed by certain other foreign-looking persons scattered about the house. Indeed, at one popular theatre the idea was later on more or less adopted, but the British artist in control was not so careful in his methods. One ardent playgoer, who was a constant visitor to this theatre, assured me that in the booking plan, hung up at that time at the back of the dress circle for the convenience of the attendants in placing those of the audience who had not previously booked their seats but purchased them as they came in, was written to a good many seats scattered about at the back and sides, which were not likely to he occupied unless the more preferable seats were full, the word 'clapper'. This gave away to the intelligent visitor the purpose and mechanism of the fictitious applause.

The other branch of this class arises from something of the same cause, but is attributable to the management rather than the artists. Their function is simply to fill as individuals empty seats at a time when business is not very good. They are in no sense paid, directly or indirectly, except by the enjoyment which, with the paying public, they may derive from the performance. By long experience it has been found that the public are in certain ways like sheep – where one goes, they all go; what one avoids, they all avoid. It is a depressing thing to see a theatre only partially filled – depressing alike to the audience and the performers; and to avoid this the management now and again is glad to welcome (by arrangement) certain unpaying guests. It is to this habit that Farmer and Henley allude in the quotation from the *Daily Telegraph* inserted in their slang dictionary found at the beginning of this article. An empty box, for instance, seen from the stage, is a disturbing influence on a player. Above the glare of the footlights the vacant box attracts his eye and takes his mind from his work – of course, to the detriment of that work.

May I say, inasmuch as I was Henry Irving's manager during the whole period of his occupancy of the Lyceum Theatre, and therefore, lest anyone should attribute to him directly or indirectly any of the practices I have mentioned, that at the old Lyceum we did not have a *claque*, though certain individuals were perpetually importuning us to engage one; and, further, that we had no need for dead-heads to fill empty seats. Of course, in all managements there are 'lean' as well as 'fat' times; but when the lean time showed signs of approach we took care to 'put on' the play always ready for presentation on the stage, and by so doing did away with all necessity or temptation to produce an extraneous appearance of public desire.

But I can say that appearance can at times be used to very great advantage. Buckstone was accustomed to use it at times during his management of the Haymarket in old days, until the 'ladies in red cloaks' were as easily understandable to the paying playgoers as were the 'Adelphi guests' who came on and went off the stage silently and with almost startling unanimity in old-fashioned melodrama. I have always understood that during the first six weeks of the phenomenally successful run of *The Colleen Bawn*, Dion Boucicault the elder 'papered the house' so effectively that, though the paying public clamoured for admission, they could not obtain seats at all until such time as the manager was satisfied that the play was assured of success. This was in one way an expensive proceeding, for expenses go on whether the audience pay or not; but it is a form of insurance, and at times well worth the cost.

Irving and Stage Lighting

Stage lighting, as we understand it now, is the growth of a comparatively few years. The one person to whom the modern cult is due is the late Sir Henry Irving. When he took into his own hands in 1878 the management of the Lyceum Theatre, the lighting of stage scenes was crude and only partially effective. But the possibilities of this branch of art had been for a long time in the actor's mind, and when he became sole master of a playhouse of his own, with undisputed sovereignty, he began to apply to it his theories and his experience, with results which dominate the whole artistic mysteries of the stage to this day. As a matter of fact, the history of the Lyceum Theatre during Henry Irving's management – from 1878 to 1898 – is the history of modern stage lighting. In 1878 he reorganised the whole theatre, which was then very much in the condition in which it has been put during Fechter's management. Fechter had in his time done much for the mechanics of the stage; indeed, the stage which he rebuilt at the Lyceum was a very elaborate affair, full of traps and appliances, but all of these requiring so many struts and supports that the space between the stage and the mezzanine floor, and between the mezzanine floor and the cellar, was of very little use for any collateral purposes – storage, passage, &c. – required in a playhouse. Irving had all this hampering matter removed in the process of time – part being done before he began the season of 1878-79, and the remainder when, in 1881, he cleared out all the rubbish left in by the builders when the theatre was rebuilt after the fire of 1830.

When the reconstruction of 1878 was in hand special care was taken to bring up to date the mechanical appliances for lighting the stage. In those days gas was the only available means of theatre lighting – except, of course, 'limelights,' which were moveable and the appurtenances of which had to be arranged afresh for every play done. But for ordinary lighting purposes gas was used; and, in order to ensure safety, certain precautions were, by Irving's direction, adopted. Instead of having all the gas to be used in the theatre – both for the stage and auditorium – supplied from one main, as had been theretofore done, he had supplies taken from two separate mains. Thus, in case of explosion, or any other cause of interruption outside the theatre, it was possible to minimise the risk of continued darkness. To this end, a by-pass was made connecting within the theatre the two supplies. Of course, an explosion in a gas main, no matter where occurring, is apt to put out all the lights fed from it – if lit. This used in those days to be the great source of danger from fire, for with the enormous number of burners in use in a theatre all turned on, and the gas escaping, the introduction of a naked light was an immediate source of danger. Thus, Irving's first care was to minimise such risk by having an immediate supply of gas available from quite another main. In the Lyceum Theatre a large number of men were employed to look after the gas, to light and turn it off as required. The rules regarding this work were very strict. Each gas-man had to carry (and use for his work) a spirit torch. Under no circumstances was he allowed to strike a match except in places suited for the purpose. After all, it was not a very difficult job to light up a scene, so far as the carrying out of the appointed way was concerned. To make this apparent to a reader not well versed in stage appliances it may be as well to explain the various mechanical appliances for lighting used on the stage:

(1) Footlights, or 'floats,' as they were called in the old days of oil-lamps, the name being retained when the applicability for it had passed away; (2) battens; (3) standards; (4) lengths; (5) ground rows; (6) all sorts of special form and size, made to suit particular pieces of built scenery.

Of these lights, the only kind directly observable by the public are the footlights. That is, they are in front of the stage, but it is essential that they be not themselves seen; otherwise their glare would entirely destroy all distinctions of light. What the public sees are the backs of the reflectors which hide the glare from the audience and send it back upon the stage. These lights are of great power. In the present time, when electric light is used for the purpose, these lamps vary from twenty to a hundred candle-power. To realise this blaze of light it must be remembered that an ordinary domestic light of the 'Swan' or 'Edison' pattern is of some eight candle-power. In Irving's time – at the close of his personal management of the Lyceum – the footlight lamps were of sixty candle-power, modified occasionally for artistic purposes, as I shall show further on.

Battens are long frames that run across the top of the stage from side to side. These contain a large number of lamps, placed side by side so as to show a very strong line of light. The battens are hung with such fittings as allow them to be raised or lowered at will. In the gas days the batten was a wooden frame to which was attached, in such a position that the light could not come into contact with anything inflammable, an iron gas-pipe, in which were fixed at regular intervals a multitude of burners. The special burners used for this purpose were what were known as 'fish-tail' burners, which allowed the flame to spread laterally, and so were, by securing good combustion, effective for lighting purposes. This gas-pipe was connected with the main by flexible leather tubes, so that provision could be made for altering the height above the stage without interfering with the supply of gas. At one end of the pipe was a burner led by quite another tube, so that it would keep alight when the main supply of that pipe was turned off. This jet was known as the 'pilot,' and was specially lit in readiness before the beginning of the play. When the supply of gas was turned on to the batten pipe, the pressure sent the flame along; for as the burners began to be fed all along the line the spreading flame of one burner caught the escaping gas from the next orifice, and in a few seconds the whole line would be alight. To ensure readiness, alterability, and safety in these and other lights, all along the stage from front to back, behind the line of the 'wings' which mask in the scene, were special water-taps connected with the gas mains of the theatre, so as to ensure a constant supply up to these points. The flexible tubes had metal ends, which fell easily into place in the taps and left no leakage. Then the gas-man with his key turned on the tap so as to make lighting possible. All these taps were so arranged that the supply at each batten could be turned on or off at the 'Prompt,' where the 'gas-table' was fixed vertically. There was a batten for each portion of the stage, from front to back. For a stage is divided for working purposes by measured distances which are the continuance of the old 'grooves' by which the 'flats' in old days used to be pushed out or drawn off. All stage hands understand No. 1, No. 2, No. 3, and so on.

The standard is a vertical pipe, set on a strong, heavy base, so as to be secure from accident of lateral pressure. The gas supply enters through a flexible tube at base, arranged with the taps in the same manner as are the battens. The top of each is a cluster of very powerful burners; thus, each standard is in itself a source of intense light, which can he moved when required.

Lengths are battens of convenient size, and are made adaptable for almost any use. As the purpose of lighting is to throw the light from front and back of the stage, these are often arranged to be hung on the back of the scenic piece in front. Hooks are provided for the purpose. Lengths can be placed in any position or shape; and, so long as their direct light is concealed from the audience, can be made to enhance or supplement any volume of light.

The ground rows are a length applied to special purpose. Stage perspective differs somewhat from the perspective of nature, inasmuch as it is much stronger; and it is therefore necessary at times to even-up this extra strength to eyes accustomed in ordinary to a different perspective focus. In fact, in proper stage lighting – that which produces what seems to be the ordinary appearance of natural forces – it is not sufficient to have all the lighting from one point. The light of nature is so infinitely stronger than any artificial light, and so much better distributed, that science and art have to be requisitioned to produce somewhat similar effect.

As to special lighting pieces for 'built' scenery, these have on each occasion to be made to serve their present purpose. In 'built' scenery it is sometimes difficult to avoid throwing objectionable shadows. The lights are so strong, and the space available is so small, that there is hardly room at times for simple effects. So, when there is a shadow which cannot be avoided, it is generally possible to build in some piece of seemingly solid work, behind which a light can be so placed as to destroy the shadow.

Now, in 1878, all this had practically to be done by gas. Of course, what are known as 'limelights' were in use. These are exceedingly powerful lights, produced by playing burning gas heavily charged with oxygen and hydrogen on a fragment of lime. This light is so concentrated that it is easily adaptable to the localising of strong light. The appliance for producing the light being small, it can be easily placed in a specially-made box, whose face is a lens of strength suitable to the work to be done. The effect is, of course, proportionate to the amount of concentration. In fact, the general scientific law applies that what is gained by direction is lost in force, and *vice versa*. In a well-equipped theatre many different kinds of limelights are now in use, the lenses being in such variety that a skilful operator can select that best adapted to the special occasion: 'open limes,' 'spot lights' of varying focus and intensity, lights so constructed as to cover a certain amount of space, and so on. The moon, the lights from the windows of the 'old home,' the convenient ray which follows the hero about the stage, so that the audience may never forget that he is present, and nearly all such aids to the imagination of the spectator are produced in this way. In '78 these appliances were comparatively rare, but the example set by Henry Irving encouraged other managers to use them, and an industry sprang into existence. New firms undertook work which had hitherto been almost a monopoly. Fresh men in ever-increasing numbers became trained to the work, and nowadays it is hard to imagine that not many years ago it was almost necessary to train workmen for this minor art.

Now as these two methods of lighting – gas and limelight – were already in existence when Henry Irving managed a theatre himself, his part in the general advance was primarily to see that both these means were perfected. To effect this he spared no expense. The equipment of the Lyceum Theatre so as to be able to use gas-light most readily and to the best advantage was a costly job. It would have been almost impossible for a layman to understand why pipes of such calibre were required for the gas of one place of business. The by-pass between the two intakes of gas – only to be used in emergency – was more than twelve inches in diameter, and the piping, fixed and flexible, throughout the building ran into many thousands of feet. But the final result was excellent. When the mechanism was complete it was possible to regulate from the 'Prompt' every lamp of the many thousands used throughout the theatre. This made in itself a new era, in theatrical lighting. By it Irving was able to carry out a long-thought-of-scheme: that the auditorium should be darkened during the play. Up to this time such had not been the custom. Indeed, it was a general aim of management to have the auditorium as bright as possible. The new order of things was a revelation to public. Of course, when the curtain came clown the lights went up, and *vice versa*. In the practical working of the scheme it was found possible to open new ways of effect. In fact, darkness was found to be, when under control, as important a factor in effects as light. With experience it was found that time could be saved in the changing of scenes. It used to be necessary, when one 'full' scene followed another, to drop a curtain temporarily so that the stage could be lit sufficiently for the workmen to see what they were doing. But later on, when the workmen had been trained to do the work as Irving required it to be done, darkness itself became the curtain. The workmen were provided with silent shoes and dark clothing, all of which were kept in the house and put on before each performance. Then, in obedience to preconcerted signals, they carried out in the dark the prearranged and rehearsed work without the audience being able to distinguish what was going on. Later on, when electric power came to be harnessed for stage purposes, this, with different coloured lights, was used with excellent effect.

Irving was always anxious to have the benefit of new discoveries applied to stage effects. In 1885, when he produced *Faust*, electricity was used for effect the first time. Colonel Gouraud (Edison's partner) kindly arranged an installation for the fight between Faust and Valentine. Two metal plates were screwed on the stage, to either of which the current of one pole was applied. One of the combatants had a metal plate screwed to the sole of the right shoe. From this a wire was carried through the clothing and brought into the palm of the right hand, where, on the rubber glove, was fixed a piece of metal. This being in contact with the metal handle of the sword – and a similar contrivance being arranged for Mephistopheles – a direct communication was established so soon as the demon's sword struck up the weapons of the combatants, and sparks were emitted.

It was not till about 1891 that electric-light was, even in a crude condition, forward enough to be used for general lighting purposes in British theatres. Irving had it then put in by degrees, beginning with the footlights, which formed a test of suitability. Electric-light differs from other lights in that when it is lowered in degree it changes colour. This is perhaps due to the fact that it is not in the ordinary sense a light at all, but a heat visible *in vacuo*. In order to allow the footlights to be turned down it was necessary in those days to have a liquid resistance which was a wasteful as well as an expensive mechanism. In addition, the light even then afforded was an unpleasing one for the stage, unless the vacuum lamps were tinted. Therefore, considerable consideration and experience were necessary before a satisfactory result could he achieved. The purpose of lowering footlights is to create a scenic atmosphere of night or mystery or gloom. Now in nature night and mystery and gloom are shown in tints of blue; but as electric light is produced by red-hot carbon the atmosphere was warm instead of cold, cheerful instead of gloomy. In those days coloured lights on the stage were in their infancy, and the best device which we were able at first to adopt was to cover the lamps of the footlights with bags of thin blue paper. This was effective, though wasteful; for, of course, in getting the colour a portion of the illuminating power was lost. In addition, though the beat of an ordinary electric globe is not very great, when the light within is of sixty or a hundred candle-power a certain amount of heat is created; and if this, or a portion of it, be retained in a paper bag there is a certain amount of danger of combustion. Of this the licensing authorities could not approve, and the device was abandoned in time to avoid trouble. In a theatre, of all places, it is necessary to remember the wisdom of the old saw: 'A well-bred dog goes out of his own accord when he sees preparations being made for kicking him out.' It may hereafter be interesting to remember that even in America, where electric lighting was in those days far ahead of what it was in England, we thought it advisable to bring – and actually to use them – a supply of blue paper bags for the footlights.

It may also be well to remember that though America has gone very fast and very far in her theatrical lighting, it only reached any considerable excellence when Henry Irving showed the stage producers what could be done. When we first visited America, in 1883, there was only one theatre there – the Boston Theatre – which had really good appliance for stage lighting. I speak here merely of the mechanism of lighting, not of the art of it. In the Boston Theatre there was a thoroughly well-thought-out scheme for the gas-lighting then in vogue. Its perfection was to be seen in the 'gas-table' in the 'Prompt,' which was then far in advance of that of any other theatre that we played in. I only quote this fact as evidence of the extraordinary rapidity with which in that marvellous land of industry and mechanism a good idea is seized on and developed to the full. At the present time a vast number of the lighting appliances for the theatre are patents of the United States, and the goods are there manufactured.

The installation of electric light in the Lyceum Theatre brought with it one somewhat cumbrous and expensive addition. Up to then the large amount of gas consumed for lighting purposes all over the house created a sufficient heat for the comfort of the audience; but so soon as electricity was used instead of gas as the main lighting, we noticed that the men of the audience began to turn up their coat-collars and the ladies to wear their cloaks. So we had to have an elaborate system of hot-water heating installed. This took some time, and till it was in working order we had to use a large number of powerful gas-stoves, placed so as adequately to heat all the passages and guard every intake of cold air.

But when once the electric current was fairly installed and the hot-water service was in working order, the old comfort was restored. The heating, which had to be combined with ventilating, was an elaborate scheme too complex to find a place in this article.

All that I have said of lighting in the theatre is merely with reference to the mechanism. The part most noteworthy, and which came from Henry Irving's incomparable brain and imagination, was the production of effect. In the seventies, as I have said, there was very little attempt to produce fine gradations of light and shade or of colour. Henry Irving practically invented the *milieu*. When he became a manager the only appliances used were what were called 'mediums,' which were woven films of cotton or wool or silk drawn between the lights and the stage or scenery which they lit. The finest stuff we then used was 'scrim,' a thin silk which gave certain colour without destroying or suppressing an undue amount of the illuminating quality. This stuff, dyed only in a few rudimentary colours, could be used to go beneath the battens and encompass the standards, wire guards being affixed everywhere to prevent the possibility of conflagration. It was also used occasionally to cover the bull's-eyes of the limelight boxes. But it was impracticable to produce colour effects, except generally. The stage could be fairly well reduced to one dominating colour, but that was all.

Accordingly Irving set himself to work in his own quiet way and, with the help of his employés, had various mechanical processes devised. He had transparent lacquers applied to the glasses of the limelights, and, when electric light came in, to the bulbs of the electric lights, and thus produced effects of colour both of intensity and delicacy up to then unknown. Instead of rudimentary colours being mentioned on the lighting 'plots' – by which the operators work – 'blue,' 'red,' &c., the plots began to direct the use of certain fine distinctions of colour, so that before long the men themselves became educated to finer work and would no more think of using 'dark blue' instead of 'light blue,' or 'steel blue' instead of 'pale blue,' than they would insert a slide of any form of red instead of any form of blue.

Then came quite a number of colours new to this use, as the possibilities of lacquer for the purpose became known and enlarged. Shades began to take the place of colours in matters of choice, and soon even the audience became trained to the enjoyment of fine distinctions of colour.

The artists who worked for the stage and who were always great admirers of the 'Chief' – or the 'Governor' as everybody called him – were very loyal to him and very willing to carry out his wishes, using for the purpose their natural abilities and the skill which they had evolved by labour and experience. Indeed, so far as I could judge, the very men who painted the scenes, and did it in so masterly a way, were glad to have him 'light' them and gave all their understanding to his assistance in the work. He in turn was loyal to his fellow artists and workers; I never knew him to fail in giving all the credit and all the honour to those by whom he was assisted.

Then, having put the matter of degree of light and its colours in good shape for use, he began to make further improvements in the artistic use of it. For instance, it was formerly usual to have the foot-lights extending in unbroken line from side to side of the proscenium arch. Now he had this line – which contained several rows of lamps of different colours – broken up into sections. Thus any combination of colour could be easily made by use of the lighting table in the 'Prompt.' By this means Irving was able to carry out a class of effects which had long been in his mind. He had noticed that nature seldom shows broad effect with an equality of light. There are shadows here and there, or places where, through occasional serial density, the light is unevenly distributed. This makes great variety of effect, and such, of course, he wanted to reproduce. An audience – or the bulk of it at any rate – always notices effect, though the notice is not always conscious; it is influenced without knowing the reason. With, then, a properly organised series of sections – both with regard to amount of light and colour of it at disposal – a greater variety of light was given to a scene. Also, as it is advisable to centre effects on a stage, it became an easy matter to throw any special part of the stage into greater prominence – in fact, to 'vignette' that part of the stage picture which at the moment was of the larger importance.

Irving also began to produce and alter effects of the combinations of coloured lights – to use the media of coloured lights as a painter uses his palette.

It was a most interesting thing to see him setting about the lighting of a scene. There were, of course, certain rudimentary matters which had to be observed in all scenes; but it may be useful to describe the *modus operandi*. This work, especially in its earlier stages – for it was a long process, entailing many rehearsals – was done at night, when the play of the evening was over. The stage workmen, after a short inter-val for their supper, got the new scene set. While this was being done, Irving and I, and often the stage-manager if he could leave his work, took supper in the 'Beefsteak Room,' which was one of Irving's suite of private rooms in the theatre. When the scene was ready he went down – usually sitting in the stalls, as the general effect of the scene could be observed better from there than from the stage. The various workmen employed in the lighting 'stood by' under their respective masters – with, of course, the master machinist and the property master and *their* staffs ready in case they should be required. There were always a large number of men present, especially at the experimental stages of lighting. The gas engineer, the limelight master, the electrician, all had their staffs ready. Of these the department most important was that of the limelights, for these lights had to he worked by individual operators, all of whom had to be 'coached' in the special requirements of the wording of the play before them; whereas the gas and electric lighting was arranged with slow care, and was, when complete, under the control of the prompter – or the masters under the direction of the prompter – who took his orders from the stage-manager. It was seldom indeed that any member of the company was present at a lighting rehearsal; never in the earlier stages. It was only when some special requirement made the presence of one of the actors advisable that such actor attended, and then only by request. The rule did not apply to Miss Terry, who, as a privileged person, could attend whenever she chose. But, as a matter of fact, she was never present at the earlier rehearsals when the scheme of lighting was invented and arranged. These were late at night, or rather, early in the morning, long after – generally hours after – she had gone home. Let it be clearly understood that the lighting of the Lyceum plays was all done on Irving's initiation and under his supervision. He thought of it, invented it, arranged it, and had the entire thing worked out to his preconceived ideas under his immediate and personal supervision. There was nobody in the theatre – or out of it, for the matter of that – who could touch or even help him. It would have prolonged his life if he could have had such help. I can vouch for this, for it was my usual practice to stay with him at such times. It was none of my business, and I was not myself a proficient; but it was a matter of absorbing interest to me to see this new branch of stage art developed, and I took full advantage of the opportunities afforded to me by my position with Irving. It was very seldom indeed that I was absent from a lighting rehearsal during the twenty years Henry Irving had the Lyceum under his sole and personal control.

In these days, when every well-appointed theatre in the United Kingdom and America has adequate appliances for proper stage lighting – electric, gas, limelight, calciums, and such other means as are adapted for special or occasional use in temporary scenic effects; flaming rosin, liquipodium, electric flashes – it is perhaps as well to think of a time when all these things were in their infancy, and to remember especially the great actor to whom the advance and the attainment of perfection were mainly due.

PART 3

Interviews

The Tendency of the Modern Stage

A Talk with Sir W.S. Gilbert on things Theatrical

[W.S. Gilbert (1836-1911) enjoyed enormous success as a dramatist and comic writer from the publication of his *Bab Ballads* (1869) to the glorious run of Gilbert & Sullivan 'Savoy' Operas which debuted from 1871 to 1896. The creation of *The Mikado* was wonderfully shown in Mike Leigh's recent film *Topsy-Turvy*, starring Jim Broadbent as Gilbert. The following article and interview took place soon after Gilbert received his long overdue knighthood in the June 1907 birthday honours list. Bram and Florence Stoker were regular visitors at Gilbert's beautiful home, Grim's Dyke, at Harrow Weald; and Florence frequently stayed with the Gilberts when Bram was on tour. The lake described in the third paragraph is where Gilbert died from heart failure while saving a young woman from drowning (in his 75th year), three years after the publication of this article. Gilbert rarely disguised his feelings for that most selfish and arrogant of actors, Henry Irving. Once asked if he had been to see Irving at the Lyceum, Gilbert replied, 'Madam, I go to the pantomime only at Christmas.' He obviously sympathised greatly with Irving's closest associate, the hugely overworked Bram Stoker. They shared many common interests, and both studied law in their earlier years.]

'In the recent Honours List,' said Sir William Gilbert, 'I found myself politely described by some Court flunkey as "Mr. Gilbert, playwright". Nine times out of ten, when a dramatic author is referred to by a newspaper man, he is described as a "playwright". The term "wright" is properly applied to one who follows a mechanical calling, such as a wheelwright, a millwright, a cartwright, or a shipwright. We never hear of novel-wrights, or poem-wrights, or essay-wrights: why, then, of playwrights? There is a convenient word "dramatist" that seems to describe fitly one who devotes his time to writing drama, taking the word "drama" in the broadest sense.'

My conversation with Sir William Schwenck Gilbert – the first knight on whom the honour was conferred purely as a dramatist – was held partly in the study of his beautiful house, and partly as we walked about the grounds of his charming estate, Grim's Dyke, at the edge of the great common some twelve miles to the north-west of London, known as Harrow Weald, part of the ancient Forest of Middlesex. The house was built some forty-odd years ago for Frederick Goodall, the painter, from the designs of Norman Shaw, the architect, who built so many fine houses in England. Mr. Gilbert – as he then was – purchased the estate in 1890. As it stands on the top of the hill, the views from it are fine. Bushey Heath marks the sky-line some three miles away to the north-west, and adjacent to Grim's Dyke is Bentley Priory, the last home of Queen Adelaide, widow of William IV.

Sir William Gilbert has made many improvements to the property chiefly in the way of adding to its picturesque effects. Among these is a pretty lake of an acre and a half in extent. Here in the summertime Sir William Gilbert and his friends swim daily, sometimes two or three times in the day. The forming of the lake was a matter of some difficulty for, as the hill is of gravel, it was necessary to 'puddle' the excavation with clay in order to make it water-tight.

Sir William supervised the doing of this himself, with the result of so severe a rheumatic attack that he had to spend some six months in Helwan [a popular health resort in Egypt] before he regained his powers of movements.

Everywhere are beautiful trees – oak, ash, chestnut, pine – with deep undergrowth of laurel and rhododendron, and many lovely dells, where the bracken rises waist high.

The house is large, and has many large and handsome rooms, all of which are stored with objects of interest and beauty. The great drawing room, which was formerly the painter's studio, and has the dimensions and windows of a chapel, is a storehouse of works of art. The fireplace, a massive carving in Derbyshire spar, some fifteen feet high, was designed by Sir William himself. On the opposite wall hangs, among many others, his portrait by the late Frank Hall, R.A. Scattered through the room are some lovely cabinets; one of great beauty, Italian of the XIVth century; another, Japanese, three hundred years old, wrought in lacquer, tortoiseshell, cedar, ivory, and agate. On one table is a great ivory goblet, German of the XVIth century; the tusk from which it was carved must have been enormous. On another table is an exquisite piece of carving in marble of a cat and kitten by the sculptor Freminet, 1863. Elsewhere in the house, scattered among works of art and curios of all kinds, are interesting souvenirs of the dramatist's own plays. For instance, in the billiard room is the block and axe used so long in *The Yeomen of the Guard*. Here, too, are hung round the walls frames containing the original drawings, done by the author, for the *Bab Ballads*: there are some two hundred and fifty of them in all. In the hall – wherein is a fine suit of steel armour – is a huge model of a full-rigged ship. It rests on a sea of green glass, and is fourteen feet long. It's a facsimile of one of the old three-deckers of a hundred and ten guns sent to the Black Sea at the time of the Crimean War – the 'Queen', in which Sir Evelyn Wood was a midshipman before he forsook maritime for land warfare. From this model, whose rigging is perfect in every detail, the scene from *Pinafore* was taken.

'W.S. Gilbert' – by which name, rather than by his new title, he is best known – is a big man of just under six feet high. As he is now in his seventy-second year, it is not to be expected that he should have retained all the burliness of his more youthful days. But the same dominant nature remains, and is expressed as of old by his masterful and militant appearance. Hair and moustache have grown white, but the face maintains its ruddy warmth. His humour is as trenchant and as quick as it has always been. Nothing is too big or too small for its mordant force. His readiness and quickness are wonderful; the occasion which another would miss is seized with lightning rapidity.

'And your own plays?' I asked. 'How many of these have you written?'

'I think the exact number is sixty-three.'

'How do you regard their respective work of the dramatist and the novelist, one against the other?'

'Their method of work is, and must be, quite different. The novelist can make his own milieu as he goes along. He can create and alter his own characters, paint his own scenery, suggest his own changes of feeling, describe effects and emotions in general terms. In fact, he appeals directly to his readers. But the dramatist cannot appeal to his audience directly; his work can only appeal through the distorting medium of many prisms. That is where we writers of plays are handicapped. We are not always masters in our houses.'

'Not even when you control the stage absolutely?'

'Not even then, though that gives us a chance. I attribute our success in our particular craft to the fact that Arthur Sullivan and I were in a commanding position. We controlled the stage altogether, and were able to do as we wished – to carry out our ideas in our way, so far as the limitations of actors would allow of it. During the years we were running new operas at the Savoy I generally had royalties on my librettos to an average of about £3,000 a year. In all, I have had somewhere about £25,000 or £30,000 on this account.'

'Roughly speaking, how many copies would that mean?'

'Well, I will leave you to work that out. I had sixpence halfpenny on each copy in London and fourpence halfpenny in the country. I suppose it averaged up about fivepence or fivepence farthing for each copy. At fivepence each this would show a sale of one million four hundred and forty thousand copies. As, however, the total amount is approximate and the royalties vary, we may, I think, call the output a million and a half.'

'What,' I asked, 'is the tendency of the modern stage?'

'Forward! Distinctly forward. In fact, from the very first, from the days of Thespis, there has been a continual development of a better class of play. There have, of course, been periods of set-back; times when all seemed to be on the down grade. But such variations occur in the development of every art. For instance, we used here in England to be largely if not wholly dependent on French plays. Indeed, in the past many of our great plays took their inspiration from foreign sources. For instance, I remember John Oxenford, the famous critic of *The Times*, telling me that *She Stoops to Conquer* was taken from a German one-act play; and that the screen scene in *The School for Scandal* was adapted from a scene in one of the plays of Calderon.'

'How about the modern French plays?'

'The French players are better than the plays. I do not care for the spirit which seems to animate modern French dramatists – most of them, at all events. Their work is almost invariably founded on broaches of the Seventh Commandment [Thou shalt not commit adultery, *Exodus* 20:14]. But the players are superb.'

'What in your opinion is the coming vogue of plays – tragedy, drama, comedy or what?'

'Tragedy is hopeless, drama has better prospects, comedy better still, farce best of all. I speak, of course, of the comparative probability of success, not of actual merit. The different forms of comedy are easier of fulfilment. We have at present a considerable number of fine comedians but few, if any, tragedians.'

'How do you account for that?'

'Supply and demand. Everybody wants comedy, but no one wants tragedy. They go to see Shakespeare's tragedies because a certain knowledge of his work is properly held to be essential to people of education. People like to be on a sort of nodding acquaintance with his plays; and so they go to see them, because to witness a performance of his plays is the easiest and the pleasantest way of acquiring a superficial knowledge of them. But in reality, in tragedy it is the actor who draws. But as the world wants comedy it has it, and fairly good comedy too. Pinero and such men have done an infinity of good in raising comedy higher.'

'How about musical comedy?'

'That is two things. As we have writers of comedy and good comedians, the prospects of comedy are bright enough. But I fear there is no composer now before the public whose work is being taken seriously by connoisseurs – if I except Mr. German, whose work is of a higher order than that of his rivals. I think this is a great pity, for the modern musical comedies serve to amuse people, even if they cannot claim to be art of a high order. They please a very large class – those who don't want to think: the shop-girl, the type-writer, the gentleman from Aldershot, and the people who make theatre parties and merely want to be amused.'

'What is your opinion about the American stage?'

'I don't care much for the class of plays that appeal at present to the American audiences. As a rule they are on the side of exaggeration, and their construction is generally inartistic. Their actors are better than their authors. That gives the play a chance, for good actors can often pull poor plays through. Authors should be grateful to players who can make their work vivid to the audience. For my own part, I have always attached immense importance to the actor's art.'

'How do you think the stage – the dramatic stage – is and is to be affected by the great popularity of the music-hall?'

'That is a rivalry in which the theatre is very heavily handicapped. The work in a music-hall is carried on under conditions which would be absolutely fatal to good work in a theatre. And then, again, the performers are different. Every performer in a music-hall is more or less a master in his craft. Not the actors only, but all who take part – conjurors, trick bicyclists, dancers and so forth. In that world it is not sufficient to be a specialist in ignorance or incompetence. A man does not go on the music-hall stage merely because he has been spun for a clerkship in a bank or has failed the Guards! The strong point about the music-hall commercially is that it only tries to amuse. There its ambition is satisfied; it does not try to elevate. My impression is that people go to places of amusement to be amused: and somehow the music-hall often fits better into the social structure than does the theatre. You need not give up a whole evening to it. It is more facile in its ways; at whatever hour you go in you can take up at once whatever is going on.'

'Do you think the theatre has a function beyond mere amusement?'

'It should have, but it rarely pays to attempt anything beyond mere entertainment. My own experience is that the higher the literary quality of the play the greater is its chance of failure.'

'Can you illustrate that – if not by the failure then by any of the things that make for failure?'

'When *The Wicked World* was produced I had to bring a libel action against the *Pall Mall Gazette*. In his summing up Mr. Justice Brett, who for the purposes of the trial had read the book of the play, said that there were some passages that would rank with any to be found in poetical drama. As illustration he read the speech from the first act beginning: "Thou hast seen black and angry thunder clouds". Now this very passage was the only one cut out after the first performance because the lines dragged.'

'There are,' I suggested, 'those who say that the public won't allow literary merit to be exercised in play writing.' He smiled – a grim sort of smile as he answered:

'If plays with a strong pretension to literary merit fail they do so not on account of that literary merit, but in spite of it. In a play the public want the story, and any departure from its strict course, introduced because the author is of the opinion that the literary excellence of the departure justifies its introduction, simply adds to its chances of failure. Some authors make the same mistake with what they call 'comic relief'. Literature belongs to the structure of a play, and not merely to its incidents. I sometimes think it would be a good thing if when a dramatist had completed his play he would read it carefully from beginning to end, and cut out all the passages with which, on account of their literary excellence, he is best pleased.'

Then, with a grim naivete all his own, he added:

'I have not always done it myself!'

Mr. Winston Churchill

talks of his hopes, his work, and his ideals to Bram Stoker

[Bram Stoker was acquainted with the brilliant young politician Winston Spencer Churchill for nearly twenty-five years. The following piece was published not long before Churchill married Clementine Hozier in 1908: Bram and Florence Stoker were guests at the wedding. Throughout his long and unique political career, Churchill hated giving interviews to anyone, so this interview was quite a scoop for Bram Stoker – mainly brought about by Churchill's great liking for, and admiration of, *Dracula!*]

(On the eve of the return to England of Mr. Winston Churchill after an African tour extending from British East Africa to the Nile, the following sketch by Mr. Bram Stoker of one of the most striking personalities in political life will be read with interest.)

When I wrote to Mr. Winston Churchill asking for an appointment to interview him he replied: 'I would very much rather not; but if you wish it I cannot refuse you.' When I met him in his library he explained more fully in words:

'I hate being interviewed, and I have refused altogether to allow it. But I have to break the rule for you, for you were a friend of my father'. Then he added gracefully another reason, personal to myself: 'And because you are the author of *Dracula*.' This latter was a vampire novel I wrote some years ago, which had appealed to his young imagination. He had himself been an imaginative writer. The first thing of his which I remember reading was a powerful short story called, I think, 'Man Overboard,' a grim, striking story wherein he followed the last thoughts of a drowning man. ['Man Overboard!' (an episode of the Red Sea) appeared in the *Harmsworth Magazine*, January 1899.]

As he had already written, some ten years ago, *Savrola*, a political novel, I asked him if he intended or wished to write others, in case, of course, he should have time to do so through the revolutions of the political wheel. He answered thoughtfully:

'No, I think not; not novels. I hoped to write, and to write as much as public life will give me opportunity of doing. But I do not think it will be fiction.

'I would rather write something in the lighter forms of history – a sort of truthful story-telling. It seems to me that the whole tendency of modern historical research is to sub-divide and prosecute investigation into each division or aspect of the matter separately. It is all done by sections. The result is not satisfactory. We used to have less details but a general picture, whereas now we get superabundant details but no general sketch, no picture or story. The work should neither be of too great length, nor should it be written for children. There is a growing opportunity for writers who will grip a subject as a whole and convey it intelligently to the plain man who wants to know but who hasn't got much time. The popularity of Fitchett's book of *Deeds That Won the Empire* illustrates what I mean'.

£25

Twenty-five pounds sterling REWARD is offered by the Sub-Commission of the Fifth Division, on behalf of the Special Constable of the said division to anyone who brings the escaped prisoner of war, CHURCHILL, living or dead, to this office.
For the Sub-Commission of Fifth Division LODX DE HAAS, Secretary.

The above, printed on poor paper in rough type, somewhat after the manner of hue-and-cry placards for runaway niggers in the bad times of slavery, was the notice which followed the escape of Winston Spencer Churchill, war correspondent, from the prison at the Model School at Pretoria in December 1899.

Seven years later the Transvaal was a British Colony and the ex-prisoner, Winston Churchill, was Under Secretary for the Colonies in the British Government; an Under Secretary who manifestly had, and was manifestly intended to have, an important share in the formation of the new Constitution of the new British Colony. 'Thus', says Feste, the jester, 'the whirligig of time brings in his revenge.'

I found Mr. Winston Churchill in his study at his pretty house in Bolton Street, off Piccadilly. The Under Secretary of the Colonies is a working man and a bachelor; the whole of the first floor usually allocated domestically for a drawing room is here utilised as a study, two rooms having been thrown into one. The houses in this part of Bolton Street are not large, and in them every inch of space is generally arranged by clever architects to practical use. The colour tone of the room is rich green, relieved somewhat gloomily by the heavy mahogany panelling and the many bookcases of the same dark wood, velvet pile carpet of green, green chairs and sofas.

The study table is a somewhat remarkable one. An immensely large and wide piece of Chippendale in mahogany with carved legs and bevelled edges richly carved; a table that seems as though it were made for the work of collating documents. Elsewhere in the double room are pretty pieced Empire furniture of tulip-wood.

The shelves are filled with a varied assortment of books, mostly editions de luxe, showing the catholic taste of the Churchill family, for very many of these editions have the book plate of Lord Randolph Churchill. Here in addition to the heavier works of history, philosophy and those bearing on politics and public life, are fine editions handsomely bound of Edgar Allan Poe, Carlyle, Richardson, Jane Austen, Dean Milman, George Grote, the Brontes, &c.

Of course, there are not here the accumulation of letters and papers; of Blue-books and files of documents which cumber up a statesman's office. All such are in his rooms at the Colonial Office and the House of Commons. Though a Minister may – and does – do much of his work in his own home, the work of this class is selected, and only such papers and authorities as are required are brought to him.

Over the fireplace in the outer room is set in the panel a fine portrait by Romney of an officer, Captain Peletan, in uniform. The windows are double framed so that the war of the elements and the roar of the traffic in the neighbouring Piccadilly can be effectively kept out. On the wall of the inner room, set so as to face one, is a lifelike portrait of Right Hon Lord Randolph Churchill.

When I came to London to be Henry Irving's manager, my acquaintance with Lord Randolph Churchill, made in Ireland, continued. Our relations were always most friendly. He often came to the Lyceum Theatre; he was a great admirer of Irving, and occasionally stayed for supper in the old Beefsteak room.

One evening at the theatre – I think it was during the long run of *Faust* – when between the acts I was waiting in the passage, I heard his voice behind me:

'Oh Bram Stoker, I want to introduce my boy to you.' I turned, and the introduction was made. Young Winston was then about thirteen, a strongly-built boy with red hair and very red cheeks. A bright-looking boy, somewhat on the sturdy side, and eminently healthy. As we shook hands the father laid his hand affectionately on the boy's shoulder, and, patting it in a loving way, said:

'He's not much yet, you know. But he's a good 'un. He's a good 'un!' And a 'good un' he turned out to be.

The son has more than fulfilled the predictions of the father. He is at this moment in the very foremost rank of living British statesmen, his dashing pugnacious methods allied to his great gifts as a speaker, his lucid power in handling public questions, and his remarkable breadth of view, distinguishing him above all his rivals.

'Why,' I asked him, presently, 'did you leave the Army? You seem to have liked soldiering and to have got on very well with it.'

'I was very happy in the Army. I did like soldiering, but the fact is that in peace time there is little if any scope in the Army for a man who wants to be active. Of course, I mean very active, and in different ways, for there is always plenty of routine work in military service. Anyhow a man must choose his own way of life, and if it is only fighting that a man wants there is plenty of that in politics. It is only by   following out one's own bent that there can be the really harmonious life.'

'Won't you define,' I asked, 'what you mean exactly by that?' He smiled. I do not think that he cares much for definitions; he makes up his mind in his own way, a way to satisfy himself.

'Harmonious life. A life when a man's work is also his pleasure and vice versa. That conjunction, joined with a buoyant temperament, makes the best of worldly gifts.'

'Why buoyant temperament? I merely ask for information.'

'Simply because it implies a lot of other things; good health and strength, for instance. The great majority of human beings have to work the greater part of the day, and then amuse themselves afterwards – if they are not too tired. But the lucky few derive their keenest interest and enjoyment not from any contrast between business and idle hours – but from the work itself. But certainly physical health has a good deal to do with it. Henry James speaks of a religion of healthy usefulness.'

'I note, Mr. Churchill', I said, 'that you use the words politics and politician where I mean statesmanship and statesman. May I take it that I am in accord with your ideas?' There was a smile on his face as he answered:

'Don't you think it would be at least unbecoming of a man to speak of himself as a statesman? Politics and politician seem to me to be very good and adequate words, quite equal to the purpose required of them. Politics are quite big enough, I assure you.'

'What, in your opinion, is the modern tendency of politics?'

'All politics in this country, and I think all over the world, are becoming divided along social and economic lines of cleavage. The movements of the past have never so operated. The Reformation secured, directly and indirectly, freedom of conscience. The English revolution and rebellion of the seventeenth century established Parliamentary government. The French Revolution achieved a very considerable measure of political equality – the idea of a national nation – citizens not separated by class prejudice; but there yet remains the greatest of all the anomalies the social and economic injustice. All politics are focussing on this.

'Perhaps it is for America to show the way. There is the naked issue between capital and labour. America's contribution to the movement for human progress will be some solution, necessarily complicated of the economic problems which confront scientific civilisations.'

The smile was not existent at the end of this guess at the future. Instead, there was a look of concentrated gravity – of deep earnest purpose, which showed something of the man within. Behind the face-mask of boyhood there came something quite different – the something which revealed a passionate earnestness not to be suspected from his general appearance. The incipient wrinkles which only show occasionally on the smooth skin of his forehead seemed to deepen, the fine lines of the well-cut mouth to harden; the eyes to get a new and earnest look.

Winston Churchill is in his 34th year, with the record of four campaigns behind him and enough memories of personal adventures to equip a Ballantyne or a Kingston. [R.M. Ballantyne and W.H.G. Kingston were two of the most popular and prolific writers of adventure stories for boys in the 19th century.] He has sat in Parliament for years and always as one of the most strenuous and daring of Members. He has borne officially the heat of the day in the new Parliament which came into the turmoil after a reign of twenty years by their political opponents. In the Commons he has been the official mouthpiece of his party and Cabinet in Colonial matters and has held himself worthily against all odds. But in appearance he is still a boy. Let us see him as he leans against the mantelpiece in his study, seemingly gay and debonnair.

Of medium height, looking rather slimmer than he is, for he is compactly built. The red hair of his boyhood has now lost some of its fire, and seems now rather a reddish brown than red. The eyes of light blue are large of pupil having in them something of the free quality of the eyes of a bird. The mouth is an orator's mouth; clear cut, expressionable, and not small. The forehead is both broad and high, with a fairly deep vertical line above the nose; the chin strong and well formed. His hands are somewhat remarkable: a sort of index to his life as well as to his general character. They are distinctly strong hands. Broad in the palm, with that breadth which palmists take as showing honesty; fingers both long and fairly thick, but tapering; the thumb slightly bent backward at the top joint. The man with such a hand should go far.

When I asked him to enlighten me as to his change of party he smiled again, but with a different one this time. It was a somewhat inscrutable smile, old Wisdom looking out of the gleeful face of Boyhood. He will, I think, take perennial delight in all that had led up to that change and in the doing of it. His words, together with the tone in which they were spoken, and that enlightening something which is conveyed by appearance, expression and manner all in unison, seemed to satisfy one's intellect.

'When I was in the Conservative party, to which I had been brought up, I was called a Tory Democrat. Even then I belonged to the progressive wing of the party. I came into Parliament after the Boer War as a representative of the high-water mark of Tory imperialism, but I was actually already in complete reaction against it. Indeed, I may say that when my change of party came there was not far to go. I went into politics on the Conservative side, just as a man might go to Oxford because his father had been there. My father was a Tory Democrat and I had been brought up in that atmosphere.'

'What is Tory Democracy?'

'The association of us all through the leadership of the past – that was what I thought it meant. It was only later on that I learned that its aspirations were exploited by the vested interests of Conservatism, simply to win the votes and popularity of working men.'

As he spoke my mind went back to a passage of his speech before the National Liberal Federation in Manchester in 1904 which seemed to link his old political faith with his new:

'We are here to sweep away the whisperings of despair. We are not going back, we are going on. Our movements are toward a better, fairer organisation of society and our faith is strong and high that the time shall surely come – and will come the sooner for our efforts – when the dull, grey clouds under which millions of our countrymen are monotonously toiling will break and melt and vanish forever in the sunshine of a new and noble age.'

Sir Arthur Conan Doyle

tells of his work and career

[The following piece is a fascinating encounter between the creators of the two most enduring figures in English literature, Sherlock Holmes and Count Dracula.

Arthur Conan Doyle (1859-1930) was a regular visitor to the Lyceum and a good friend of both Henry Irving and Bram Stoker, who presented Doyle's first play, *A Story of Waterloo,* to great critical acclaim at Bristol in September 1894. 'To my own mind *Waterloo* as an acting play is perfect, and Irving's playing in it was the high-water mark of histrionic art', declared Stoker. In the same year as *Waterloo's* premiere, Doyle's classic novella of psychic vampirism, *The Parasite,* was published as the first volume in Constable's Acme Library series. The second and companion volume was Bram Stoker's *The Watter's Mou'*.]

'My first book! That was written when I was six years of age! But if I am to tell you about myself, I suppose I had better start at the beginning.'

The speaker was lying on a chintz covered sofa in the pretty drawing-room of his house at Hindhead, down in Surrey. The forenoon sun was streaming in through one of the mullioned windows, of which the bars were softened by the delicate fringe of green of the creepers which spread all along them. The whole room was full of soft light, which showed the fine old furniture and the multitude of dainty knick-knacks to perfection. Even the many quaint and pretty pictures seemed to stand out from the walls.

Conan Doyle built his house Undershaw in the western angle at the joining of the road from Haslemere with the Portsmouth road, just below the very top of the hill. It stands on a little platform lying below the road. As north and east of it is a thick grove of trees and shrubs, it is completely sheltered from stranger eyes except from down the valley.

The 'interview' which followed was the result of many questions. The subject of it was most kind and amenable, thoroughly understanding everything and willing to enlighten me as required. But he is not naturally a pushing man or an egotist, and it was necessary to keep him resolutely to the point of his own identity. I say this as his various statements were so lucid and illuminative that I think it better to give them in his own words in the sequence of a direct narrative. After all, there is nothing like a man's *'ipsissima verba'* to show the reality of the individual through the mistiness of words. I omit questions except where necessary, and only venture to add comment or description where such may add to the reader's enlightenment.

'My people on the father's side,' said the creator of Sherlock Holmes, 'were all artists of a peculiarly imaginative type. My father, Charles Doyle, was, in truth, a great unrecognised genius. He drifted to Edinburgh from London in his early youth, and so he lost the chance of living before the public eye. His wild and strange fancies alarmed, I think, rather than pleased the stolid scotchmen of the 50s and 60s. His mind ran on strange moonlight effects, done with extraordinary skill in watercolours; dancing witches, drowning seamen, death coaches on lonely moors at night and goblins chasing children across churchyards.'

All these pictures were in the room, or in some of those adjacent. With them were a host of others, delicate fancies and weird flights of imagination. There was one tiny picture of a little fairy carrying a branch and leading a beetle by a string, which was daintily sweet.

'I have myself no turn for that form of art at all beyond a very keen colour sense which makes a discord of shades perfectly painful to my eyes. I suppose, however, that there is a metabolism in these things, and that any sense I have for dramatic effect corresponds, or is an equivalent in some degree to the artistic nature of my father, whom, by the way, I in no degree resemble physically. But my real love for letters, my instinct for story-telling, springs, I believe, from my mother, who is of Anglo-Celtic stock, with the glamour and romance of the Celt very strongly marked. Her I do resemble physically, and also in character, so that I take my leanings towards romance rather from her side than my father's. In my early childhood, as far back as I can remember anything at all, the vivid stories which she would tell me stand out so clearly that they obscure the real facts of my life. It is not only that she was – and still is – a wonderful story-teller but she had, I remember, an art of sinking her voice to a horror-stricken whisper when she came to a crisis in her narrative, which makes me goose-fleshy now when I think of it. I am sure, looking back, that it was in attempting to emulate these stories of my childhood that I first began weaving dreams myself.

'When I was six I wrote a book of adventure – doubtless my mother has it yet. I illustrated it myself. It must be an absurd production but still it showed the set of my mind. When I went to school I carried the characteristic with me. There I was in some demand as a story-teller. I could start a hero off from home and carry him through an interminable succession of wayside happenings which would, if necessary, last through the spare hours of a whole term. This faculty remained with me all my school days, and the only scholastic success I can ever remember lay in the direction of English essays and poetry. I was no good at either classics or mathematics; even my English I wrote as pleasure, not as work.

'After leaving Stonyhurst I was sent to a "finishing" school in Germany, the Tyrol. There again my tendency to letters asserted itself. I started and edited a school magazine. Although the German acquired was indifferent, I think I had great benefit from the small but select English library. Macaulay and Scott, I remember, were my favourite authors. But I was and am still an omnivorous reader, with very catholic sympathies. There is hardly anything which does not interest me. Indeed, it would be difficult to name any form of true literature that does not give me intense pleasure.

'In 1876 I drifted into the study of medicine. The reason largely was that my people lived in Edinburgh' – he pronounced the word in Scotch fashion, 'Edinboro' – 'and there is a famous medical school there. For four years I went through the curriculum. My people were not at that time wealthy, and it was a struggle to keep me at college. So I compressed my classes into the winter and devoted each summer to serving as a medical assistant, and so earning a little money to help to pay the fees. I served in this way in Sheffield, in the country districts of Shropshire, and finally in Birmingham – a billet to which I returned three times. The practice lay mostly in the slums of that great city, and I certainly saw a large variety of character and of life, such as I could hardly have known so intimately in any other way.

'The only trouble to me in this arrangement of my life was that I had no means of gratifying the love of athletics which was very strong within me. I used to box a good deal, for that consumed little time; but my cricket and football were neglected. I can say, however, that I have played for my university in both cricket and Rugby football. I had then no time or chance of being a constant player; I feel justified, therefore, in taking it out at the other end. I played a heavy match at football when I was 42 years of age and I still, at the age of 48, play cricket twice a week. So I claim now the debts which were not paid to me in my youth.

'When I was nearly 21 a friend of mine who had been a surgeon to a whaler in the Arctic seas told me that he was unable to return that summer, and offered me the billet. I was away for seven months in the Greenland ocean. I came of age in eighty degrees north latitude.

'This was a delightful period in my life. There are eight boats to a whaler and the eighth, which is kept as a sort of an emergency boat, is manned by the so-called "idlers" of the ship. These consisted, in this case, of myself, the steward, the second engineer, and an old seaman. But it happened that, with the exception of the veteran, we were all young and strong and keen; and I think our boat was as good as any.'

As he spoke he could not fail to remember the harpoons hanging on the staircase wall. They seemed to account for this enthusiasm. He went on:–

'One of the truest complements I ever had paid me in my life was when the captain offered to make me the harpooner as well as surgeon if I would come for another year. When you think that a whale was then worth some £2,000, and that hit or miss depends on the nerve of the harpooner, I am proud to think that the skipper, old John Grey, should have offered me such a post.

'On returning home from the Arctic I took my degree having been thrown back one year by the fact of going North. I was 22 when I qualified and, thanks to my numerous assistantships, had a very varied experience behind me.

'Almost immediately afterward I was offered the post of surgeon on a steamer going down the west coast of Africa. I was again most fortunate in my captain and the voyage was a delightful one. We were away four months, and the pleasure of my experience was only marred by my getting a rather virulent fever which prevails on that coast. Two of us got it, and the other man died, so that I suppose I may call myself lucky.

'On my return to England I settled in practice, first in Plymouth and then, after a few months, at Southsea, the fashionable suburb of Portsmouth. My adventures in that rather romantic period, and all my mental and spiritual aspirations, are written down in *The Stark Munro Letters*, a book which, with the exception of one chapter, is a very close autobiography.

'In this period my literary tendencies had slowly developed. During the years of my studentship my life was so full of work that, though I read a great deal, I had little time to cultivate writing. After starting in practice, however, I had much – too much time on my hands; and then I began to write voluminously.

'For ten years I wrote short stories; roughly from 1877 to 1887. During that time I do not think that I ever earned £50 in any year by my pen, though I worked incessantly. Nearly all the magazines published the stories anonymously – a most iniquitous fashion, by which all chance of promotion is barred to young writers. The best of those stories have since been published in the volume called *The Captain of the Polestar*. Sometimes I saw my stories praised by critics but the criticism never came to my address. The *Cornhill Magazine*, *Temple Bar*, and *London Society* were the chief magazines in which my stories appeared.

'Finally in 1887 I wrote *A Study in Scarlet*, the first book which introduced Sherlock Holmes. I don't know how I got that name. I was looking the other day at a bit of paper on which I had scribbled "Sherringford Holmes" and "Sherrington Hope", and all sorts of other combinations. Finally at the bottom of the paper I had written "Sherlock Holmes." *A Study in Scarlet* appeared in a Christmas number of Beetons Annual. The book had no particular success at the time, though many people have been good enough to read it since.

'My next book was *Micah Clarke*, a historical novel. This met with a good reception from the critics and the public, and from that time onward I had no further difficulty in disposing of my manuscripts. When two years later I wrote *The White Company* I felt that my position was strong enough to enable me to give up practice. I still cling to my profession, for I came to London and started as an oculist. After six months, however, this also seemed unnecessary and I finally retired. I have not indulged in my profession since, except when I went campaigning.'

That he did good service in that noble profession in the South African war is attested not only by his book on the record of the Langman Hospital, but by a noble silver bowl which stands at a corner of his house in Hindhead, on which is inscribed:–

'To Arthur Conan Doyle, who at a great crisis – in word and deed – served his country'.

How Mr. Pinero writes plays

Told in an interview by Bram Stoker

[The celebrated dramatist Arthur Wing Pinero (1855-1934) was the son of a Jewish solicitor, whose family was of Portuguese origin. Abandoning a law career, he made his stage debut in Edinburgh at the age of 19, then served as an actor with Irving's Lyceum Company for five years from 1876 to 1881. Following his first 'hit' as a writer, *The Money Spinner* (1880), Pinero wrote a long run of successful comedies and farces, notably *The Magistrate* (1885), *The Schoolmistress* (1886), *Dandy Dick* (1887), *Sweet Lavender* (1888), *The Cabinet Minister* (1890) and *The Amazons* (1893). In 1893, with *The Second Mrs. Tanqueray* (starring Mrs Patrick Campbell; and generally considered his best play), Pinero forsook comedy and began a period of realistic tragedies which were received with enthusiastic acclamation and made him the most successful playwright of his day. Among the best of his later successes were *The Notorious Mrs. Ebbsmith* (1895), *Trelawney of the Wells* (1898), *The Gay Lord Quex* (1899), *His House in Order* (1906), *Mid-Channel* (1909), *The Big Drum* (1915) and *The Enchanted Cottage* (1922; filmed by Hollywood in 1945). Pinero's plays have continued to be very popular long after his death. The London stage revival of *The Magistrate* with Alastair Sim (perfect casting!) in 1969 was enormously successful. Pinero was knighted in 1909, a year after Stoker's interview. Stoker and Pinero remained friends for over thirty years, following their first meeting at the Lyceum in 1879. "How proud I am to count myself amongst those who have the privilege of your acquaintance," wrote Pinero, after Stoker dived into the Thames in an attempt to save a drowning man in September 1882.]

I found Pinero in his London home, a charming flat overlooking old-fashioned Hanover-Square. The study where we met looks over the square to the south, and the roar of London traffic comes modified by height, but still existent.

Pinero has also a charming place in the country. An old farmhouse, 'Stillands,' at Northchapel, Sussex. This house has also an important bearing on the author's work as will be seen.

The centre of both these places is the striking figure of the great dramatist himself. A man of a little more than medium height, not in any way stout but not abnormally thin; of well-knit, capable frame: a figure that suits a horseman, a bicyclist, a golfer, for Pinero is all of these and some others. He is quite an expert bicyclist.

His head and face are both peculiar and striking. One could never fail to recognise him in the flesh, having once seen his portrait. He is extremely bald, so that there is no mistaking his craniological peculiarities. A head something like an enormous egg. A masterful face, whose main characteristics are of insight, astuteness, and above all subtlety. His forehead falls back over an enormous frontal sinus, that ridge of bone above the eyebrows which phrenologists take to mean a 'power of distinguishing slight differences': which being applied to use becomes practically knowledge of character. His eyebrows are wide and thick and strong, indeed of such size and manner as to become a necessary part of caricature and even of the delineation of exact character.

'How do you set about writing a play?' I began.

'The "setting about" is fairly uniform, though the writing is various. I must tell you that to me the theme and the working out of it are very different things and require quite different settings. I must start the theme in a city. I must have life around me – eager, strenuous, pulsating life. It may be in a crowded thoroughfare. It may be here in my own room at night, with the sense of life around me: with the hum and roar of movement and traffic coming up to me from below. It is only when such is around me that my brain quickens to creative work. Later on, when the theme is accepted, and the general scheme seems to take cohesive shape, the method of work entirely changes. I have to get away somewhere all by myself, where I shall have nothing and nobody to interrupt me.'

'Do you work all day long?'

'Not at all. My actual day's work at the play is three or four hours. That is quite as long as the mind can remain fresh and is content to be concentrated. When the mind is getting wearied it becomes rebellious to details – and a play is all details.'

'Is it all the same to you in what part of the day you work?'

'No! I do not work in the early morning. My time is at night or in the late afternoon. Perhaps I ought to explain that this is not altogether a matter of choice, but one of habit. In my early years of writing, while I was still an actor, my hours were of necessity late. In the morning I was rehearsing or studying my part; then, after the early dinner which is necessary in the routine of an actor's life, I rested to prepare for my night's work. Therefore, my only time, the only time I could depend on for play-writing, was late at night.'

'Do you know, and can you say, why it is that retirement is necessary for your working out your ideas?'

'I think it is because my work is impersonal. In the play I am not, in anything I say, speaking for myself. I am merely the mouthpiece of the various characters; and that I may understand and follow out each character of each constantly varying conditions of mind I have to be able to hold myself in some sort of abstraction, uninfluenced by external conditions. One's own personality, you see, is apt to interfere in the work if one is constantly being reminded of it.'

'Do you find your work influenced – helped or hampered – by your experience as an actor?'

'That is a big question, and certain things have to be explained before it can be answered. On the one hand, I should say that the dramatist who has been an actor is better able than others to overcome the difficulties of the craft; on the other, too intimate an acquaintance with the theatre and its associations is apt to narrow a man's view of life – to beget mere theatricalism. On the whole, however, practical experience of the actual theatre is of advantage to the playwright. It shows him, if he has eyes to see, that anything can be done on the stage by the man who knows how to do it.

'Yes, the art of the stage is illimitable. I read in some modern criticism of limitations of the stage. But to me there are limitations only of the author's capacity to deal with the technical difficulties of the medium in which he has undertaken to work. Stevenson wrote that drama is falsification of life. That was because he never took pains to acquire the necessary theatrical technique. No! there need not be falsification, though there must be compression. A drama is an epitome; but because a thing is small in bulk it also is not necessarily imperfect. Perfection is not the attribute of size.'

'In writing a play do you think of the powers and idiosyncrasies of the actors who are to play in it?'

'No; I try to dismiss from my mind all thought of the theatres, of actors and actresses. The theatre is to me then a building only. There is no thought of the individual players until the play is conceived and in great part written. After all, you know, if a writer while doing his work thinks of certain performers he will be all out in his calculations if those special persons do not play it.'

'Do you alter much as rehearsal?'

'Never! I never alter anything. All that we call "business" is in the printed matter which I carry into the theatre. Why should it be altered when it has all been carefully and even laboriously thought out, every detail of it, during the process of construction? The movements of a man and what he has to say are inseparable. Expression is multiform and simultaneous. To alter one phrase is to weaken all. I try to think of these things beforehand. Rehearsal is not – or certainly should not be – a time for experiment. It is to prepare for the acting together of the players, not for the making of the play.

'Speaking to any young writer for the stage, I would caution him against composing what is called a "rough draft" of the play first and holding himself bound by it. An elaborate scenario is carpenter's work, and belongs to a lower form of composition.'

'But is there no received mechanism or formality of thought or method in playwriting?' I asked in order to get him to talk on, not to challenge his statement.

'With every play I write I have to learn afresh the art of playwriting.'

'Indeed! Are there, then, no binding principles in this art?'

'There are binding principles, but there are no binding methods. It is the method that I have always to learn afresh!'

Why? Does each subject regulate its own treatment?

'Just as in real life no two lives are exactly the same, and cannot be recorded in exactly the same way, so in fiction. Stories of different people, different events, cannot be told with efficacy on a similar plan.'

'Am I to take it, then, that there are no sharp edges at the bounds of dramatic art?'

'There are no bounds – except, of course, those to suit the demands of the special case. There are properly no bounds of art at all, and to force the adoption of settled formula would be fatal.'

He went to one of the bookcases and took down a quarto volume bound in white vellum. Turning the pages over rapidly, he began to read:-

'"I don't want to be oracular, but I do remember the immutable law of variety. Nature seldom condescends to replicas. You may roam the whole world, as I have, and you won't discover two noses that are absolutely a match. ... How much more striking is the diversity when you get under the skin, when you touch disposition, mood, talent!"'

'What is that from?' I asked.

'That is the way I tried to put my idea on the subject in *His House in Order*.'

'Do some themes which suggest themselves prove on trial their own unfitness?'

'Certainly. But that belongs to the conceptive, the experimental, the tentative side of work. You may take it that you can do anything you wish on the stage. But the choice is a matter of your own artistic conscience in the first place. And in the second place the quantity and quality of your skill in the service'.

'By the way, I suppose in play construction there is some sort of rule, just as in building a house, though all the details may vary?'

'Of course there is. There are lots of rules, but most of them can be classed under one head.'

'And that?'

'Logic. I am a thorough believer in logic. There is no art without it. The groundwork of a play, as well as of its character, must be logic. Cause – effect! Cause – effect! The pendulum swings between the two. Two of the most substantial parts of the fabric which go to make up a fine play are logic and intuition. Without the first you can't construct a play. Without the second you can't write it!'

'Where does intuition come in?'

'It furnishes the points of view. You, a man, are perhaps writing of a woman, and you must look from her point of view. It was what enabled Shakespeare to create Portia, Beatrice and the rest of his wonderful women. It was understanding, principally.'

'Do such parts as those you mention help actors to rise to them?'

'Good parts make good actors. That is, they reveal the powers that are latent or unknown. The parts do not create the powers. A power is, after all, a power even if it be not conscious.'

'You spoke of the pendulum swinging between cause and effect. Does it swing dramatically in any other way? For instance, between comedy and pathos, or tragedy and commonplace, or character and hard fact?'

'Not as a method, but only if situation calls for it. There are very often occasions when such contrasts are the perfection of good art and are most effective when they present themselves. But to drag them in is vile. A self-conscious artist is no artist at all!'

'Before we part I want you to say, if you don't mind, what you think of the progress of American art?'

'I say with the greatest pleasure, and quite freely and sincerely, that dramatic art in America is advancing by leaps and bounds.

'The audiences? Oh, to my mind the American audience is the most intelligent in the English-speaking world. I love America and Americans. This I say in spite of the fact that I have received from them at times, as I believe, some injustice. Yes, the change in America is what is going on all over the world; the change from classic and romantic drama to naturalism'.

'And what is your opinion to continuous advance?'

'There is no such thing as continuous advance. You must go back occasionally. When a man wants to take a second plunge into the water he has to get out and remount the plunge-board [diving board].'

'How do you think the new school will be affected by the National Repertoire Theatre that we hear of?'

'I hail it with delight; I only hope the news is true. If its aims and methods justify what we are told, it will render a service to not only American home-grown drama but to British also. In fact, all drama will benefit. It will help, in my view, to show that there is already in existence a very fine English drama – that is, an English-speaking drama.

'Everything can improve, and will improve. There is nothing to prevent it. I read a great deal about the obstacles put in the way of the creation of good modern drama. But I know of no cause operating against the production of fine modern drama upon the English-speaking stage, except the disinclination or the inability of the modern dramatists to write it!'

Pinero has a habit, perhaps won from his acting days, of unconsciously suiting his action to his words. As he spoke the last paragraph he moved quickly about the room. At the last he put on a pair of heavy gold-rimmed spectacles. It seemed as though he were looking for some of those elusive obstacles.

Mr. De Morgan's Habits of Work

The career of a man who began to write after he was sixty-four years old

[William De Morgan (1839-1917) spent most of his life as an innovative and brilliant designer and manufacturer of ceramics, especially tiles and stained glass. He was regarded by many as the greatest potter of the 19th century (comparable to Josiah Wedgwood and Bernard Leach in the 18th and 20th centuries respectively).

His first novel, *Joseph Vance* (1906), clearly written under the influence of Charles Dickens, was an enormous success. *Alice-for-short* (1907) was another popular bestseller. This described a little orphan adopted by an artist. As she grows up, an old mystery surrounding the haunted house in which they lived is revealed. M.R. James, a great admirer of this novel, commented: 'I never cease to admire the skill with which the ghost is woven into the web of the tale: that is a very rare feat'.]

'I was brought to novel-writing first by the desire to do a thing which I thought I could not do. For sixty-four years of my life – so long as was possible – I waited. Then I tried. In 1904 I made the experiment with what is now the first chapter of *Joseph Vance*. That chapter, as it now stands, is exactly as it was first written. I was diffident about it, and put it aside. Later in the year, when we were going to Florence, it came with us amongst a great mass of business papers. My wife read it in Italy, and was sufficiently pleased with it to advise me to go on. When I attempted to develop further the incipient story, I found the task a very pleasant one; and when Lossie came into it I began to get deeply interested. In this spirit I went on with the book, and finished it. I did not then think of publishing it.

'By the way, the story that got into the press here is substantially correct; that of the head of the typewriting office who complained that her girls were always reading the manuscript and weeping over it, instead of going on with their work.

'The original idea of the story was that it should be a story told by an old man in a workhouse. It was to be the story of his own life, and on its bare, bald, material side was that of Joseph Vance. There was, however, no sentiment in it of any kind, no humour, no brightness anywhere. But the original conception in that form was impossible – too unutterably sad for any form of picturesque reproduction. There was in reality no such old man – except in my own imagination.'

The speaker was William Frend De Morgan, the author whose first two novels, *Joseph Vance* and *Alice-for-short*, achieved such instant and great popularity both in England and in America. The above enlightening statement is a memorandum made of a pleasant chat in his picturesque old home at Chelsea, England. Mr. De Morgan is extremely reticent – indeed almost shy – in speaking of himself and his work. It was only in answer to direct queries that he would unfold anything of himself or his memories. But he is a most kindly and genial man, and of very sweet and sympathetic nature, as indeed any reader of his charming work can discern for himself or herself. As we chatted in his little study looking out into a garden, large for a house so near the heart of London, his natural diffidence wore away and he revealed himself. New light came into his mind from old memories; illuminating thoughts expressed themselves in an atmosphere of colour. This is natural enough in a man who had spent forty years as a worker in picturesque designing and manufacture.

When I asked him if either of his published novels was in any way reminiscent of persons or incidents, he told me that, so far as he could recollect, the character and life of Charles Heath in *Alice-for-short* was largely reminiscent of his own life as a student. 'With the exception,' he added, 'that Charles did more work!'

Of the characters in *Joseph Vance*, he said that, when he read it over after its publication, 'I found that I could pick out little bits here and there which were real and were either personal to myself or things coming within my knowledge of others.' Then he made a statement, quickly but with a sincerity which there was no doubting:

'But there was no real Lossie! She came me in the book, as though she belonged there. She really seemed to step out into my literary life, just as the girl in the story did into Joseph Vance's.'

With this foothold as to the mechanism of his literary mind, I asked him if, in his work, the various combinations of characters required thought and consideration on his part, or if they in any way seemed to combine themselves. He answered at once:

'Hardly so. I had a great struggle to get *Joseph Vance* coherent at the end. I really thought at one time that I had got into a muddle from which there could be no extrication. Happily that was not so with *Alice-for-short*. In that case all went through very easily.'

'I suppose,' I ventured to suggest, 'that the power of plot-making develops with exercise and experience?' He smiled as he replied:

'That is so, as far as my experience carries me. In my first book that branch of the art of novel-writing was wrought out by the sweat of my brow. I had to think of everything, consider everything, foresee everything, so far as 1 could. But even then there was a sad lot of loose ends and ragged edges; all of these had to be carefully laboured over till some sort of unity of idea of the whole thing was achieved, in so far as it was in me to do it. When I began *Alice-for-short* I found the value of all this labour. Things began somehow to settle themselves, and to fall into line in a natural way. It seemed to me as if the mechanical power of my mind was getting adjusted to its new work.'

'Do tell me something of yourself?' I asked.

'My father, Augustus De Morgan, author of the *Budget of Paradoxes*, was professor of mathematics at University College for forty years. All the books on this shelf were written by him.' Here he opened the glass door of a bookcase standing beside the window and showed me a whole row of works whose backs and covers showed signs of time and wear. 'Here is the *Budget*. It is a record of all the circle squarers and longitude finders. A sort of history of all the scientific 'freaks' and 'cranks' and such like.

'My mother was the daughter of the Rev. William Frend, who left the Church of England to join the Unitarians. Later on he became an actuary – one of the first of that calling; so you see that, he, too, was a mathematician of no mean order. He did the actuarial work for the Rock Insurance Company. That was about two years before Waterloo. Here is a work of his, *Evening Amusements*, written late in his life. So that, also, may be a hereditary trait in his grandson. You can guess how far back he went when I tell you that he was Second Wrangler and Smith's Prizeman nine years before the French Revolution.'

'And your own education?' I queried, for it seemed that this subject should follow next in sequence.

'I went to school and college at University College, Gower Street. Then I drew at Cary's old school in Bloomsbury. This Cary was the son of Cary the translator of Dante. My schooling there was before 1859. From that I went to the Royal Academy Schools. I was then twenty years of age, having been born in November 1839. I worked at the Academy schools up to 1863 or 1864, when I began to devote myself to stained glass and afterwards to ceramics. This last was in 1872. I did not commence to write books till 1904. I could never, I should say, call myself a painter.

'The artistic work which I carried on for so many years was what is now known as the De Morgan Lustre and Persian ware. In its own way it was, I may say, quite original. But I have no right to claim invention or reinvention of lustre. The method of doing this had been rediscovered in Italy in 1856; and many pieces of this ware were exhibited in the Exhibition in Kensington in 1862. This exhibition of 1862 was a sort of echo of the Great Exhibition of 1851. It was at that time intended to have a repetition every tenth year; but in 1861 things were not quite ripe for it, and so it was postponed for a year.'

'Did your plastic ability ever take any other form than that of ceramics?' I asked. He answered me with a smile.

'I have often made inventions, if that is what you mean!'

'Tell me some of them?' I asked.

'I think the most important was a new duplex gearing for a bicycle.

This is actuated pneumatically. There are two independent gears, wheels, and chains. By pneumatic force one gear is changed to another, without any appreciable amount of friction being generated. This I protected; and I kept the patent alive as long as I could afford it. But after I had spent some £300 on it, I allowed it to lapse. I was surprised as well as disappointed that no manufacturer took it into use, for it is a really good idea.' He took me out through the garden to a sort of lumber-room, and there showed me a bicycle geared in the way of the patent. It is a really admirable scheme, and I think it must yet come into use. This particular setting was of the earlier pattern. There is a separate gearing on each side of the frame, high on one side, low on the other; but he has since arranged both to be on the right-hand side, so that they can be enclosed in the same gear case. At the end, on each side of the handle-bar, is a rubber bag; squeezing one makes the wheel cease to be 'free,' the other changes the gear. When we returned I asked him:

'Have you made other inventions?'

'Oh yes, lots of them; but none commercially successful. Perhaps the most important were: First, a sieve for refining large masses of clay; this I used in the pottery work with great success. Another was a smoke-consuming firegrate. But these things I have let slide since I have devoted myself to literature as a pursuit, which I trust to follow for the remainder of my days.'

'May I ask you,' I suggested, thus happily recalled to the main subject of my visit, 'as to your character-creation? Do your characters come from your brain full-fledged, or do they grow from small beginnings and become more and more real as the story progresses?'

'The latter altogether. So far as I can remember, for it is hard to recollect the exact beginnings of characters, the process is a sort of nebulous idea, with a concrete heart somewhere in the mist. A heart which can from the first illuminate in some degree, and which can beat in time and grow more and more and more vital, till at the last it emerges from the mist. And then, strangely enough, you are not astonished when you find that the creature which has newly declared itself is a friend of your lifetime, of your dreams. When this point is reached the characters often act and even speak for themselves. At times it seems as if one can almost hear their very words.'

'Do they ever,' I asked, 'get away from you at this stage; do they ever take, so to speak, the bit in their teeth and bolt?' Once again he smiled that understanding smile which is the sign of sympathy; that smile which Mrs. Riddell, author of *George Geith of Fen Court*, described a generation ago as 'beginning at the eyes and spreading to the rest of the face.'

'I wouldn't undertake to say that they don't; and I must say that I don't object when they do. For this often leads to a new line of thought.

It seems to me often that it is such divergences that make for the freshness of a story. After all, if the characters are true to nature, with just that touch of individuality, even if it be eccentric, which makes people interesting in real life, they can give a charm of their own in literature. And if these fictional characters have fictional life, why should they not use it fictionally in their own way? We talk, now and again, of imaginary characters as 'living.' Surely it is this quality, if any, which makes them so!'

Mr. De Morgan has a most interesting physical personality. He is in height about six feet, though this seems lessened somewhat by his tale of years. He is of slight build, with shoulders square. His head is well balanced on a fairly long neck; sign of high type. It is well shaped; very wide and full behind the ears, with bold forehead, wide between those ridges which phrenologists call the 'bumps of imagination.' These manifestations are sufficiently marked to be noteworthy. The top of the forehead rises in a steep ridge of bone, manifestly of considerable strength, for it once resisted, without evil effect collaterally, a blow from the swingback of a heavy door which stripped away the skin. The eyebrows are fairly thick, but nothing out of the way. His hand is characteristic – the fine, dexterous, sensitive hand of an artist skilled in plastic work. He has a strange story to tell of a prediction, based on the lines of his hand, made long ago and since justified. But this he wishes to tell himself in his own way and at his own time.

He lives when in London, for he spends most of his time now in Florence, in an old-world corner of Chelsea. His home is one of the few survivals of an older period; one might almost call it the 'rural' period of Chelsea. And even it is doomed, for its time is coming for alteration. 'The Vale' is an eddy of the stream of the King's Road, the great East-and-West thoroughfare of that part of London. In itself it is secluded, but the roar of traffic passes over the line of houses which stretch between it and the great highway. The shriek and roar of the motors and the pounding of horses' feet on the hard asphalt come modified and almost muffled. But they come; and when such sounds are strenuous and perpetual, within their radius is no place for art. The house is a fairly old one, all ramshackle, with some queer little rooms and alcoves made in the process of 'improvements' at various times. It is just such a house as should be found in a quiet suburb. Attached to it is a large studio used by Mrs. De Morgan who, in her maiden name of Evelyn Pickering, made distinguished success with her pictures, as she has done ever since. She was one of the exhibitors at the first exhibition of the 'Grosvenor Gallery' in the early 'eighties.' She has also exhibited at the New Gallery. A year ago she had a 'one-man' exhibition at Bruton Street which was criticized most favourably by the press. She also exhibited at Dresden, Cologne, and other foreign cities in turn. One of her pictures, 'Life and Thought,' from Tennyson's poem, 'Life and Thought Have Gone Away,' is in the Liverpool Art Gallery.

Here, in the studio, by the half-light of the coming evening, are seen many of her pictures or easels. They represent her specially imaginative school of work. Her subjects are varied, and the names given them explain generally their meaning: 'The Gilded Cage,' 'The Cadence of Autumn,' 'The Hour Glass,' 'The Light Shining in the Darkness,' 'Port after Stormy Seas,' ' Eve in the Garden of Eden.'

Throughout, the house is full of beautiful and interesting things. It is quite a storehouse of artistic curios; among them are many of Mr. De Morgan's own ceramics, works of supreme and delicate beauty.

Before I came away I asked Mr. De Morgan to tell me something of his method of work. I compress his answers to my queries into a single statement. I mention this lest it should seem egotistical on his part to say so much of himself. This would be an unjust suspicion of anyone; but especially in his case, for he is the most modest of men. I look on it as a grave courtesy on his part that he broke through his natural timidity far enough to answer so many of my seemingly impertinent questions.

'I make no scenario. I just go on finding, as one often does, such inspiration as is necessary from my pen. I find that the mere holding of a pen makes me think. The pen even seems to have some consciousness of its own. It can certainly *begin* the work. Then I forget all about it, and go on wheresoever thought or the characters lead me. I think I work best in Florence, where it is always quiet and where there is something stimulating in the air. It is certainly stimulating to the nerves; perhaps it is to the intellect also. I work there all the winter through. My time for beginning work is after breakfast. I work all day, off and on, and sometimes a little in the evening. Weather does not affect me, as all my work is done indoors.'

Having mentioned the subject of America to him, he said, and said with considerable feeling:

'It has been an extraordinary pleasure to me to find that, Britisher born and raised as I am, I can still find American readers. I assure you that the receipt of assurances to that effect from remote regions out West that were still in the wilds when I was old enough to read Fenimore Cooper and Catlin have been to me a matter of rejoicing and bewilderment. All the more, because it shows that politics and geography have completely failed in making foreigners of two halves of a divided race that speak the same language, and will do so as long as each adopts the neologisms of the other as fast as they come from the mint!'

PART 4

Miscellaneous

The Great White Fair in Dublin

*How there has arisen on the site of the old Donnybrook Fair
a great exhibition as typical of the new Ireland as
the former festival was of the Ireland of the past.*

The great white city which has arisen as if by magic in Herbert Park,
Dublin, is in itself a revelation to British eyes. There have been many
exhibitions in the United Kingdom since the days when the Crystal
Palace stood in Hyde Park, but never a one has been able to boast such
architectural uniformity, such general fairness of outline. In other
countries they may do these things better, but the British builder
learns new tricks slowly, and the secrets of massive palaces of seeming
white marble, which are built almost in a night and as speedily taken
away, are only now becoming familiar to him. It is safe, therefore, to
predict that when his Majesty the King visits the Dublin Exhibition
during the coming summer, he will find an outlook which for brillian-
cy and beauty has never before been equalled in these isles. Given a
clear sky of Irish blue and a soft summer sun, one could well imagine
oneself in the heart of Italy, or even in the still more luminous atmosphere of the Orient.

As is usually the case in most undertakings of this character, there
has been a great deal of controversy and recrimination in the course of
its completion, but it is sincerely to be hoped that after the gates of the
great Fair are opened on May 4 [1907] by the Lord-Lieutenant in full
state, all bitterness will pass away, and that there will remain full
opportunity for a general expression of Irish pride in an object so worthy to evoke it. These gleaming mansions, green lawns, and brilliant
flower-beds, standing on the borders of a blue lake, crossed by beautiful bridges, are such as to make glad the heart of every artistic, sentimental Irishman. It is a far cry from this glittering vista to the latter
days of the Donnybrook Fair, which forty years ago was accustomed
to make this neighbourhood ill-famed throughout the world. The contrast is perhaps characteristic of the Ireland of yesterday and the
Ireland to-day, which this Exhibition, and, in a smaller way, this number of *The World's Work*, seeks to celebrate. The days of Donnybrook
Fair and all it meant, the days of the stage Irishman and the stagey
Irish play, of Fenianism and landlordism are rapidly passing away, if
they have not even now come to an end. Perhaps there has been some
joy of living and humour lost with the passing of the country fair, its
merry-makings, its rows and its shillalahs; but there has come in its
place a strenuous, industrious spirit, spreading its revivifying influence so rapidly over the old country as to be worth more than even

historical bitterness and sentimental joys. Patrick's problem is fast finding its solution in divers ways. Perhaps the many visitors to Ireland whom this Exhibition will attract will be astonished to find here, and outside in the country at large, what wonderful things are being done to start the island upon a new career of industrial progress, aside and beyond affairs political. And if this Exhibition does nothing else than call the attention of the world to this new spirit abroad in an old land, it will serve its purpose well.

But there are other purposes which it will serve – for instance, it will introduce Patrick to his new self.

If the value to a country of an International Exhibition is to be measured by the educational facilities thus afforded to its people, there is probably no section of the British dominion which could take from it so much benefit as Ireland can. The geographical position of the island, which stands as the outpost on the Western sea; its isolation, emphasised by the neglect of many centuries; and, from the nature of its natural products, a logical lack of transport facilities – all have tended to create for its inhabitants a personal ignorance both of itself and of the outside world. So, too, the great world beyond has become aware of its identity only through external causes; to only a comparative few of the great bulk of international travellers is the country personally known. And so it is that the functions of such an Exhibition are to make known the whole to each of its parts, with the added opportunity of studying by comparison the conditions, resources and progression of other countries, and of making the country and its work known to other peoples who on such an occasion visit it for purposes of pleasure or business. Inasmuch as Ireland is naturally an agricultural country, the lives of its people are, as a rule, spent in narrow areas. A scattered population can never have the same facilities of travel as one which is mainly grouped in great centres. Again, in aggregations of necessity small, art has little chance for display or development; the lessons of the imagination have few expansive opportunities, and a whole world from which art workers may be drawn remains barren. Through the duration of an exhibition, large numbers of persons of all classes must attend. Special efforts in the way of transport are made, and inducements of all kinds offered; the very existence of such an undertaking has a concentrating effect; a national centripetal force is generated to which an extensive and varied public willingly yield themselves.

Ireland has certain natural advantages which have largely yet to be exploited. In agriculture, all growths can flourish which depend on soft air, moisture, and deep soil. The surrounding seas abound with fish of every kind. The mineral possibilities are as yet but little known; but there are vast areas of fuel-bog, sufficient alone for national wealth.

The newcoming captains of industry need not undertake their fresh responsibilities heavy-hearted. Already there are proofs of the industry and suitability of the people in manufactures, where such have been undertaken. Indeed, the complete stranger who investigates may be surprised to find here already some individual industrial undertakings, the largest and most successful of their kind in the world.

From the very start, therefore, the originators and organisers of this International Exhibition have – and must have – felt themselves justified in their undertaking. They had, of course, to contend with an initial difficulty consequent on the poverty of the country. For, after all, Ireland is poor, and its population, possibly from political causes, has dwindled in the last sixty years to a little over one-half of its former number.

To any one who has known Dublin in or before the fifties [1850s], the change made in this locality during the interval is amazing. At that period it was more or less of an uninviting waste on the ragged edge of an unimportant stream, best known as the site of Donnybrook Fair. Founded more than seven hundred years ago, in the time of King John, it fulfilled for some centuries a useful economic function; but in time it degenerated into a place of such rowdiness that its very name became a synonym for misconduct. I remember an expression which I often heard used of it in my own youth: 'The Devil would be in Hell only for Donnybrook.' At last it became so notorious an evil that it had to abolished.

Now on the spot where it flourished has risen, for the purposes of national and international good, a 'Lordly Pleasure House,' organised and arranged for the display of the direct and indirect results of learning, science and art, and illustrative of that progress which follows in their wake. More than fifty acres have been devoted to this beneficent and ennobling work, laid out in such a way as to afford in the simplest manner proper classification of the various exhibits.

Dublin stands at the head of a magnificent estuary shut in to the south by an amphitheatre of mountains, and as the main entrance of the Exhibition faces north, the visitor approaching or within the grounds sees the great range of snowy domes and pinnacles standing out stark against the rising hills and towering into a sky of Irish blue – a blue which an American enthusiast poetically compared with 'a colleen's eyes'! The entrance building is a huge one, containing a great Concert Hall capable of seating over two thousand people, and a series of Dining and Refreshment rooms sufficient to entertain a vast number of persons. The long corridor through this building, which is in the nature of a bridge, for it crosses a street, is decorated with views of Irish scenery, and allows of a number of minor exhibits and of those little kiosks and stalls for the sale of souvenirs which are so popular with the larger class of visitors. The southern side of this section faces a great garden where, in the centre of the grounds, is the 'Grand Central Palace,' a huge building in the style of Italian Renaissance from which stand out four great wings. The centre of this forms a great hall large enough to contain even the greatest concourse of visitors likely to attend at any one time; it is of a diameter of over two hundred feet. It is topped by a dome nearly a hundred feet across and a hundred and fifty feet high.

The architecture of this great hall is simple, but it is fine and chaste and of very considerable artistic merit. The extending wings are well proportioned and adapted to their purpose. A pretty effect with a national bearing is produced by the ends of the supporting beams of the roof, which are so shaped as to represent *en masse* a cluster of pendent shamrocks.

At the north-western side of the grounds stands the 'Palace of Industries.' The section is mainly technical. The 'Palace of Mechanical Arts' is an immense building nearly a thousand feet long, occupying more than a third of the entire length of the grounds. At the eastern end of it are power-producing appliances of different kinds. Here, doing active service, are facsimiles of the furnaces of the battleship Dreadnought. Here, too, are the great engines and dynamos for producing the lighting of the Exhibition. The other sections of this great building are those of machinery in motion, engineering, and transportation.

At the eastern end of the building, and facing the lake, is the 'Palace of the Fine Arts,' a building of chaste severity in the Florentine style. In its five halls, occupying a floorage of some thirty-five thousand feet, are to be found works of art of all nations, but naturally the most important section is that devoted to Irish art.

This section consists of three categories of works of art : (a) Those selected from works sent by their authors in response to a general invitation made to 'Artists of Irish Birth or Extraction.' (b) Works sent by living Irish artists of distinction in response to individual requests. These include fine specimens of the works of John Lavery, Charles Shannon, J. J. Shannon, William Orpen, George Henry. There is also a selection from the works of the late Walter Osborne. (c) A number of fine examples of the work of the artists of the older Irish school. Some of these have been lent by the National Gallery and some by the Tate Gallery.

A section is devoted to Sculpture, and grouped sections are illustrative of the work of Irish engravers and deceased Irish miniature-painters.

There is, in addition, a very extensive and representative collection of works by British and Foreign Painters and Sculptors, among which are hosts of works whose titles, as well as the names of the painters, are household words.

One of the most striking features of the Exhibition is the great pavilion erected by the Canadian Government. In it are exhibited not only specimens of Canadian productions – minerals, cereals, and industries – but a grouping of stuffed specimens of the fauna of the Dominion.

One section is devoted to 'side shows' of various kinds, a huge water-chute, the largest yet built in this country, a switch-back railway, a helter-skelter tower, and many other forms of more or less active amusement such as are loved by the ordinary visitor.

The general appearance of the grounds is very attractive. Wherever it has been possible, the trees already existing have been allowed to remain, and many others, of course of lesser growth, have been added. A lake has been dug out, and forms a pleasing feature of the general view, and will doubtless prove an attractive feature of the pleasure section of the Exhibition.

The World's Greatest Shipbuilding Yard

*Impressions of a Visit to Messrs. Harland and Wolff's
Shipbuilding Yard at Belfast*

It would be difficult to imagine any better object-lesson to a country
from the point of view of commercial enterprise than the magnitude,
stability, and prosperity of Harland and Wolff's shipbuilding yards.
The founders and developers have proved beyond all doubt that success is not necessarily dependent on natural local conditions. In Belfast
the shipbuilding industry has to depend solely on labour – labour
based on thought and enterprise. In the process of turning out fleets of
the finest vessels afloat, there is, in a word, no aid from local natural
products.

Less than fifty years ago the firm of Harland and Wolff was a small,
unambitious concern. It was only when the manager, Mr. – afterwards
Sir – Edward Harland acquired possession, that expansive power
began to manifest itself. It was not, however, till Lord Pirrie took command that full development was reached. For close on forty years he
has been connected with the firm, first as partner, latterly as head.

In this shipyard it is possible to follow the whole process of construction, from the reception of the raw material, in itself a big work,
to the departure of the registered ship. All day the sound of clattering
metal is heard on the stone pavement of the Queen's Road; great wag-
gons are carrying lengths of flat or angle steel. Brass, copper, lead,
iron, tin, and even costlier metals pass along. There comes also an endless procession of tree-trunks – English oak and Irish ash; paint; rubber; cement; canvas; goods for upholstery in every form; and in addition to raw material, anchors and chains, cables and hawsers of steel
or hemp or coir, ventilators, lamps, and electric and other fittings.

The works may be divided broadly into two sections: first, the shipyard proper where the 'ship' is put together; and secondly, the different series of stores for raw and completed material, power-houses,
workshops, and administration buildings. In the latter section the tim-
ber is dealt with in its various stages. There are acres devoted to the
preparation of this material alone: ponds for steeping (for certain
woods require to be 'seasoned' in various ways), and sheds for drying
both in bulk and in cut form.

Here may be seen fine-grained yellow pine from Canadian slow-
growing forests, great teak balks from Rangoon; enormous trunks,
roughly squared by the axe, of giant mahogany from Honduras; hard-
woods of beautiful texture and pattern, suitable for panelling and
veneering, from Californian mountain woods, from Pacific Islands,

from tropical rivers. The odour of the dry dust of yellow pine and the damp dust of teak blend and give a strange and unique aroma to the place.

The other great building in this section is that devoted to the boiler shops. The main building is no less than six hundred feet long. The boilers for the great ships are of huge size and thickness of steel, fortified by enveloping bands of inch-and-a-half steel.

In this area of the yard are also the pattern-shop, stores, fitting-shop, spar and riggers shed, sail-loft, and boat-shed. The newest building in the section is the electric generating station – in itself an example of up-to-date perfection.

The shipyard proper is surrounded on three sides by water; to the south the Abercorn Basin, to the north and west the River Lagan. On the south end are five slips – always occupied – and on the north four, and no sooner is a vessel launched than preparations begin for laying the keel of another.

Perhaps the most remarkable of many remarkable things is the perfection of the establishment's organisation – no slight matter in an industry where the type of work is constantly changing, and where weights and measurements grow by leaps and bounds. At the north end of the yard the space has had to be increased by adding the low-water shore and making it available by shutting out the tide with coffer-dams.

There are in the yard three enormous travelling gantries, viz., vast bridges supported by tressels, which move on rollers working on firmly laid rails. On these the cranes lift and shift material for the ship beneath. These gantries cost something like £25,000 each, so that the widening is an elaborate and costly undertaking. Yet at the south end of the yard has lately been erected a still larger gantry costing perhaps as much as four of the older pattern. The bridge is stationary, 600 ft. long, and supported by mammoth uprights. Along this works the travelling double or 'bridge' crane, whose top is 185 ft. above ground. It is wide enough to cover two great ships, one on each side. By electric power it lifts any weight and deposits it where required. It travels the whole length of the bridge in one minute. It is so arranged that if only one side of the crane is working, or if one is carrying a heavier weight than the other, a supplementary weight travels automatically on the other side so as to keep even balance. In addition to the traveller, this bridge has supplementary cranes, also movable, from which are suspended the hydraulic riveters, which now play so important a part in iron structures. For some purposes the ordinary riveter's hammer is not sufficient, and the hydraulic riveter is used. It is an immense double mass of steel, shaped like a lobster's claw. When the points are adjusted, pressure is applied, and in an instant the great fiery bolt is squeezed into a solid mass inextricably one with the plates it holds.

The first operation in building is, of course, the laying of the keel, already drilled with holes for riveting, to which are bolted the various ribs already prepared. Then along its centre is fixed a single sheet of steel plating, some four feet high, making one of the divisions between the double bottoms of the ship. From the keel bottom other plating is curved, and this spreading upward and outward fixes the base-lines of bow and stern. Amidships the plating is carried out laterally as the ship's bottom is here quite flat.

Close in front of the slip lying alongside the sea-wall is one of the latest ships launched from the yard, and as yet the largest. She is being 'finished,' and three thousand men are at work on the job. She is the new White Star boat *Adriatic*; 708 ft. long, beam 75 ft., gross tonnage 24,000. Her engines alone weigh 3,000 tons, and when her captain stands on the bridge he will be a hundred feet above the keel.

There are at present nine great ships on the stocks in this yard ranging in length from 400 to 650 ft. with corresponding tonnage of 6,000 to 23,000. For many reasons a ship is not nearly complete when she leaves the slip. For the output of a yard is limited by the number of available slips. And even in an incomplete state the weight of a great ship is such as to create an exceeding difficulty of movement. When the *Great Eastern* was launched there were many unsuccessful attempts before she could be moved; the snapping of a hawser under the terrific strain put on it resulted in a large death-roll. Since that time, however, much has been learned. Now the actual keel does not slide at all; it is the casing under it which slides, and this in a trough of tallow.

The mere appearance of these vessels towering over one makes one exclaim, 'Here we undoubtedly find Efficiency.'

The very yard itself is an instance, and no mean one, of human endeavour. Originally a slab formed by the embouchment of a river on a tidal shore, it had in itself but little stability, and was not used for any work of magnitude. It was known as Queen's Island. Then it became a pleasure garden with small zoological annexe. As in its existing capacity it had to be prepared for the reception and sustaining of vast weights, it had to be banked and built up on every side. Embedded in its depths are thousands and thousands of piles, representing an enormous sum of money and an incredible bulk of material. The labour and expense of pile-driving on such a gigantic scale must have been immense. It is such investment of capital – investment made with forethought and boldness – to which is due the success of great enterprises. Shipbuilding as a venture at the outset must always be expensive.

All through this great shipyard, the biggest and finest and best established in the world, there is omnipresent evidence of genius and forethought; of experience and skill; of organisation complete and triumphant. In the doing of this great work – so various, so interdependent

– all seems simple, whether it be in perfected details or vast combination. The building of a ship appears to be mere child's play.

Some twelve thousand men are employed here all the year round. At half-past five o'clock on Friday afternoon a horn blows, and section by section the men line up outside the score of pay-offices. At twenty minutes to six the last man passes out with his salary. As there are twelve thousand people employed at an average weekly wage-bill of £20,000, the payment of these varying accounts within ten minutes instances the perfection of business organisation, which can hardly be exemplified in a better or more fitting manner.

The Censorship of Fiction

There is perhaps no branch of work amongst the arts so free at the present time as that of the writing of fiction. There are no official prohibitions, no embarrassing or hampering limitations, no oppressive restraints. Subject and method of treatment are both free. A writer is under no special obligation, no preliminary guarantee; he may choose his own subject and treat it in his own way. In fact, his duty to the public – to the State – appears to be *nil*. What one might call the cosmic police do not trouble him at all. Under these conditions, hitherto possible by the self-respect of authors, a branch of the art of authorship has arisen and gone on perfecting itself in mechanical excellence, until it has become an important factor of the life of the nation. To-day if the supply of fiction were to be suddenly withdrawn the effect would be felt almost as much as the failure of the supply of breadstuffs. Happily fiction is not dependent on the existence of peace, or the flourishing of trade, or indeed on any form of national well-being. War and business worries – distress in any form – are clamorous in their own ways for intellectual antidotes; so that though the nature of the output may be of every varying kind, the supply is undiminished. Herein it is that the wide scope of the art of fiction proves its excellence; as no subject and no form of treatment is barred it follows that changing needs may find settlement in suitable opposites. And so imaginative work becomes recognised in the higher statecraft as a useful product.

But in the real world all things are finally relative. There is in reality, whose existence and progress must be based on cosmic laws, no such thing as absolute freedom. The needs and necessarily recognised rights of individuals and groups must at times become so conflicting that some sort of give-and-take rules or laws are necessary to the general good. Indeed we might put it in general form that freedom contains in its very structure the germs of restraint. The measure and method of that restraint have to be ascertained by experience, and in some measure by experiment, for if we wait till experience, following a simple course of *laissez faire*, has learned the worst that can happen, at least a part of the protective force of common sense is thrown away.

This is a philosophy too simple to be put in books, and has its existence in the brain of every sane individual. Let us apply it to the subject in question – the union or at least the recognition of two values, the excellences of imagination and of restraint. Restraint may be one of two kinds – either that which is compelled by external forces, or that which comes from within. In art the latter in its usual phase is known as 'reticence.' This is the highest quality of art; that which can be and is its chief and crowning glory. It is an attribute practically undefinable. Its conditions are so varying and so multitudinous, its degrees so finely graded, its workings so mysterious, its end so elusive, that it is not possible to explain it adequately by words which are themselves defective and yet of ever-varying meaning. Suffice it that it is recognisable, and recognised, by all true artists. In it consists largely, if not wholly, the ethics of art; and on it, or in it, depends that quality of art which brings it within the classification of 'high' art. The measure of the ethics of the artist is expressed in the reticence shown in his work; and where such self-restraint exists there is no need for external compelling force. In fact, self-restraint is the bulwark of freedom, inasmuch as it makes other forms of restraint unnecessary. Some power must somewhere in the advance of things recognise the imperfection of humanity. When the integer of that great body recognises that imperfection and the evils consequent upon it, those evils are at their least.

This is especially so where imagination is concerned, for the bounds of such being vague, the restraint from within need only be applied to the hither or known edge of the area of demarcation; whereas if laws of restraint have to be made at all they must, in order to be of efficacy, be applicable to the whole area. This proposition may seem at first glance to be in some way a paradox; that as the object of the external power is to prevent a thing of possible good from straying into the region of evil, the mandate should be to prevent excursion beyond the outmost point of good. But it is no paradox at all. The object is not merely to prevent the straying from the region of good but to do so with the least measure of effort and at the smallest cost of friction. Whatever law, then, can be made or whatever application of force used to effect this – whether such law or force originate from within or from without – should in the first be as little drastic as possible and in the other as gentle as may prevail. Indeed, the difference between the internal and external forces thus applied is something like the difference between ethical and criminal laws. In the great world of fact, if ethical law be not observed the criminal law must come into operation, so that the balance of individual right be maintained and cosmic law vindicated.

I think this may be proved by the history of two great branches of fiction – the novel and the drama. By drama we must take drama when acted. Unacted drama is but the novel in another literary form. The novel we must accept in its old meaning as a story, quite irrespective of length or divisions. In the case of drama the necessity for an external controlling force has been illustrated throughout some three centuries, and by its history we may by a parity of reasoning gain some light upon the dangers of the other form of literary effort. Of course, primarily the controlling force comes into operation because the possibilities of trouble are multiplied by the fact that its mechanism of exploiting thoughts is by means of the human body; and inasmuch as poor humanity is likely to err in many ways, possibilities of error in this respect are superadded to the inherent possibilities of purely literary form. There is also another aspect of this control which must be mentioned before being set aside, lest it confuse issues in the case of the novel. This latter is the State aspect of censorship. It must be borne in mind that this is a State and not a political aspect. It came into existence and remains entirely for the protection of the King. The official who has to deal with the question is a State and not a political official, and has his bounds of jurisdiction regarding drama fixed *ipso facto* by the residence of the King. But in the matter of the general welfare of the public the censorship of the drama is based on the necessity of perpetually combating human weakness. This weakness is of two kinds – or rather in two forms: the weakness of the great mass of people who form audiences, and of those who are content to do base things in the way of catering for these base appetites. In fact, the quarrel rages round the standard of the higher law, made for the elevation as against the degradation of humanity; another instance of the war between God and devil. The vice of the many of the audience in this case is in the yielding to the pleasant sins or weaknesses of the flesh as against the restraining laws made for the protection of higher effort. The vice of the few who cater is avarice pure and simple. For gain of some form they are willing to break laws – call them conventions if you will, but they are none the less laws. The process of this mutual ill-doing is not usually violent. It creeps in by degrees, each one who takes a part in it going a step beyond his fellows, as though the violation of law had become an established right by its exercise. This goes on till a comparison between what was and what is shows to any eye, even an unskilled one, a startling fact of decadence. Then, as is too often observable in public matters, official guardianship of ethical values wakes up and acts – when it is too late for any practical effect. To prevent this, censorship must be continuous and rigid. There must be no beginnings of evil, no flaws in the mason work of the dam. The force of evil, anti-ethical evil, is the more dangerous as it is a natural force. It is as natural for man to sin as to live and to take a part in the necessary strife of living. But if progress be a good and is to be aimed at in the organisation of national forces, the powers of evil, natural as well as arbitrary, must be combated all along the line. It is not sufficient to make a stand, however great, here and there; the whole frontier must be protected.

> For while the tired waves, vainly breaking,
>   Seem here no painful inch to gain,
> Far back, through creeks and inlets making,
>   Comes silent, flooding in, the main.

What use is it, then, in the great scheme of national life, to guard against evil in one form whilst in another form it is free to act? In all things of which suggestion is a part there is a possible element of evil. Even in imagination, of whose products the best known and most potent is perhaps fiction, there is a danger of corruption. For imagination is not limited to materials of a special kind; there is no assorted and approved stock of raw material for its use. The whole worlds of fact and fancy are open to it. This is its strength, and those who have imagination and believe in its power as a working factor in education – and so making for good – may well be jealous of its privileges, not the least amongst which is its freedom. Its weakness on its assailable side is that it is absolutely and entirely personal. To what Walt Whitman calls the '*en masse*' imagination does apply, does not appeal. If the '*en masse*' feels its effects it does so not as a unit but as a congeries of individuals; a wave there may be, but it is a wave of integers dominated by a common thought or purpose. This being so, the strongest controlling force of imagination is in the individual with whom it originates. No one has power to stop the workings of imagination, not even the individual whose sensoria afford its source. But the individual producer or recorder can control his own utterances; he may have to feel, but he need not of necessity speak or write. And so individual discretion is the first line of defence against such evils as may come from imagination – itself pure, a process of thought, working unintentionally with impure or dangerous material. To the drama as written this argument applies; to the play as acted it does not. The dramatist like any other person of imagination can control his output in the first instance. And like any other writer he has been, up to the present, free to print his work; his publishing it being simply subject to ordinary police control. It is on the stage and acting side that the censorship as existing comes in. Of course it must be borne in mind that if the evil is traceable to thoughts as set forth in words, the words must then come into the purview and under the knife of the censor. But up to the point of stage use the dramatist has the same freedom as any other writer of fiction.

Now as to the possible evils of imagination. Wherein or of what kinds are or may such be? We shall, I think, on considering the matter, find that they are entirely limited to evil effects produced on the senses. Here I speak only on the ethical side; there may be evils of revolt against political or social laws, but in such case the work of imagination, novel or drama, must be taken as an educational machine or medium only. Imagination does not appeal to a nation except through its units, and so must be taken as dealing with individuals only, though its effects may ultimately become of general, if not of universal import. As example, in a base play given in a crowded theatre, though many may be gratified and so debased by the exposition of lewd suggestion – either verbal or of movement or appearance – there are others who will be disgusted. It is through the corruption of individuals that the harm is done. A close analysis will show that the only emotions which in the long run harm are those arising from sex impulses, and when we have realised this we have put a finger on the actual point of danger. Practically in this country the danger from unacted plays has not up to the present existed. English people do not as a rule read plays; they prefer to see them acted. This is no doubt largely due to the fact that for a couple of centuries the plays that have been published, having already for stage purposes passed the censor, have had any passages considered objectionable or suggestive of evil deleted. As a practical matter they are as a rule but dull reading to those who look for salacious matter. Truly even the plays of the Restoration period and after, when Congreve, Wycherley, Farquhar and Mrs. Aphra Behn flourished, were written to suit a debased public taste; even these are but tame affairs compared with some of the work of our novelists. But if the growing custom continues of publishing as literary works stage plays forbidden for that purpose by the censor, the public may – will – end by reading them in the hope of finding offensive matter. They will bring to the study for evil motives an ardour denied for purposes of good.

I may perhaps here explain that I speak of 'the censor' for purposes of clearness and brevity. We have a certain censorship over plays, but there is no such official as 'the censor.' By the Theatres Act the work of supervision of the stage is entrusted to the Lord Chamberlain, and it is a part of the duty of that functionary to issue the licence decreed by the Act as a necessary preliminary to the production of the play in a licensed theatre. For convenience – since he naturally cannot do such a mass of work himself – the Lord Chamberlain deputes a well-qualified gentleman to make the necessary examination of the plays submitted for licence. It is this gentleman to whom is applied the term 'censor' by the writers of letters to newspapers and of articles in magazines who clamour against 'oppression' and call aloud for absolute freedom of subject and treatment of stage productions.

Here we come to a point at which for our present purpose we may speak of 'fiction' as containing both the forms of imaginative fiction, the novel and the drama. If we take it as 'published' fiction we can exclude all considerations of the drama, as the word fiction will include all sorts of literary effort as applied to imaginative work, of which the drama is but an accepted form. Henceforth in this article we must take fiction to mean published fiction, irrespective of form or size. By this means the matter narrows itself down to its simplest form, and we find ourselves face to face with the question: Are we or are we not ultimately to allow fiction to be put forth without any form of restraint whatever? The question is not merely a civic or national one.

It is racial, all-embracing, human. Fiction is perhaps the most powerful form of teaching available. It can be most potent for good; and if we
are to allow it to work for evil we shall surely have to pay in time for
the consequent evil effects. Let not anyone with a non-understanding
or misapplied moral sense say or believe that fiction, being essentially
based on something that is not true, should be excluded altogether
from the field of morals. The highest of all teachers and moralists,
Christ Himself, did not disdain it as a method or opportunity of carrying great truth. But He seemed to hold it as His chosen means of
seeking to instil truth. What is a parable but a novel in little? A parable may be true in historical fact – its ethical truth may be complete,
but if so the truth is accidental and not essential. When those who lis-
tened to the Master were told that 'a sower went forth to sow,' or that
'a certain man planted a vineyard, and set an hedge about it,' or 'a certain man made a great supper, and bade many,' or 'two men went up
into the Temple to pray,' did they believe, or were they intended to
believe, that they were being treated to a scrap of veracious history?
No. The purpose of the Teacher was to win their hearts through the
force of imagination. If there be any doubt about this, read the parable
of Dives and Lazarus. Here the Master, who knew the workings of
heart and brain, did not hesitate to give even presumably fictitious
details which might enhance the force and conviction of His story –
just as a novelist of to-day does. He followed the two men into the
divisions of the 'under world,' and even heightened the scenic effect
by the suggestion of a great gulf between the two. When Christ taught
in such a way, are we to reprobate the method or even to forego it?
Should we not rather encourage and protect so potent a form of teaching, and guard it against evil use?

The first question then is as to restraint or no restraint. That
restraint in some form is necessary is shown by the history of the last
few years with regard to works of fiction. The self-restraint and reticence which many writers have through centuries exercised in behalf
of an art which they loved and honoured has not of late been exercised
by the few who seek to make money and achieve notoriety through
base means. There is no denying the fact nor the cause; both are only
too painfully apparent. Within a couple of years past quite a number
of novels have been published in England that would be a disgrace in
any country even less civilised than our own. The class of works to
which I allude are meant by both authors and publishers to bring to
the winning of commercial success the forces of inherent evil in man.
The word man here stands for woman as well as man; indeed, women
are the worst offenders in this form of breach of moral law. As to the
alleged men who follow this loathsome calling, what term of oppro-
brium is sufficient, what punishment could be too great? This judgment of work which claims to be artistic may seem harsh, and punishment

may seem vindictive; the writer has no wish to be either harsh or vindictive – except in so far as all just judgment may seem harsh and all punishment vindictive. For look what those people have done. They found an art wholesome, they made it morbid; they found it pure, they left it sullied. Up to this time it was free – the freest thing in the land; they so treated it, they so abused the powers allowed them and their own opportunities, that continued freedom becomes dangerous, even impossible. They in their selfish greed tried to deprave where others had striven to elevate. In the language of the pulpit, they have 'crucified Christ afresh.' The merest glance at some of their work will justify any harshness of judgment; the roughest synopsis will horrify. It is not well to name either these books or their authors, for such would but make known what is better suppressed, and give the writers the advertisement which they crave. It may be taken that such works as are here spoken of deal not merely with natural misdoing based on human weakness, frailty, or passions of the senses, but with vices so flagitious, so opposed to even the decencies of nature in its crudest and lowest forms, that the poignancy of moral disgust is lost in horror. This article is no mere protest against academic faults or breaches of good taste. It is a deliberate indictment of a class of literature so vile that it is actually corrupting the nation.

The subject is one seriously undertaken, and with a full sense of responsibility. The evil is a grave and dangerous one, and may, if it does not already, deeply affect the principles and lives of the young people of this country. The measure of protection from it involves a departure from the custom of free speech hitherto tolerated by the Legislature. But the class it deals with is constructively a criminal class, and repressive measures such as are required in dealing with all crimes are necessary. Press criticism, which might help to restrain, is sadly deficient; the Press generally has manifestly not done its duty in this respect. The offenders are such as are amenable only to punitive measures. They may be described as a class which is thus designated in the searching Doric of the North of Ireland, 'They would do little for God's sake if the devil was dead!' It is hardly possible to obliterate such works of shameful lubricity; unhappily the weakness of poor humanity makes a continuous market for them. But we should at least try to prevent for the future such filthy and dangerous output. We take steps to deal drastically with evils that menace the well-being of society. Dance houses are regarded jealously, disorderly houses are sternly dealt with, the sale of noxious drugs is carefully regulated, even the sale of intoxicants is limited by restraining measures. In fact, all occupations based on human frailty are by the general wisdom of the State put in greater or less degree under supervision. Why not, then, if necessary, adopt the same attitude towards an evil more grave than any of the above, because more insidious?

The writer does not, for one, wish such a thing as a censorship of fiction to be brought about if it can be possibly avoided, if some other means of protection for the highest class of literature can be found or designed. He glories, like the others of his calling, in the freedom of letters, and trusts that some way may be found of dealing with the dangers that threaten. But if no other adequate way can be found, and if the plague-spot continues to enlarge, a censorship there must be. Of course there is, in a way, a remedy already. There exists a censorship of a kind, but it is crude and coarse and clumsy, and difficult of operation – the police. No one could wish an art so fine as literature, with a spirit as subtle and evanescent as oenanthic ether – the outward expression of the 'thaumaturgic art of thought' – put under repressive measures carried out by coarse officials. But it is the coarseness and unscrupulousness of certain writers of fiction which has brought the evil; on their heads be it.

The sad part of the whole thing is the wantonness of it. Coarseness there has always been of some measure. Smollett, for instance, was undeniably and wantonly coarse; even Fielding's beautiful work was dyed with the colour of an age of luxury and unscrupulousness. But certain of the writers of our time claim absolute freedom of both subject and method of treatment, in order that they may deal what they call 'problems.' Now there is no problem which may arise to any human being in the long course between the cradle and the grave which need be forbidden to public consideration, and which may not be wholesomely dealt with. There is not a household which may not have its painful experiences of some of them, and they are solved to *some* end with boldness and decorum. But it may be feared that writers who deal with lewd subjects generally use the word 'problem' either as a shelter for themselves or as a blind for some intention more base than mere honest investigation. The problem they have in reality set themselves is to find an easy and prosperous way to their desires without suffering from public ignominy, police interference, or the reproaches of conscience; with the inevitable result that they rightly incur the penalties distributable by all three. It is the same old problem which has tortured fallible humanity from the beginning, or, at any rate, since desire of many things found itself face to face with inadequate powers and insufficient opportunities for attainment.

Truth can always investigate in worthy fashion. Otherwise medicine and surgery would be obnoxious trades, and law and the administration of religion dangerous callings. As it is, those who prostitute their talents – and amongst them the fairest, imagination – must expect the treatment accorded to the class which they have deliberately joined. The rewards of such – personal luxury and perhaps a measure of wealth – may be theirs, but they must not expect the pleasures or profits of the just – love and honour, troops of friends, and the esteem of good men.

The American 'Tramp' Question

and the old English Vagrancy Laws

The 'Tramp' question is eternal. No age or country has been able to solve it satisfactorily, for the idle of each age and nation more or less adapt themselves to surrounding conditions. At the very start the matter requires differentiation: to separate those who are by nature idle from those who are poor by circumstance. It may be of some service to compare, with regard to this matter, the circumstances of England before and up to three centuries ago with those existing to-day in the United States of America. Up to the middle of the sixteenth century rural England was much very much in the same circumstances as rural America to-day. We must, of course, leave out the facilities of movement, which are very different; but this latter advantage is largely in favour of the vagabond. According to Froude, the population of England was in the middle of the sixteenth century somewhere about a million persons. In this he probably underestimated to a great degree, but his statement will serve as an illustration; the figures really do not matter. The population was scattered largely amongst little villages and hamlets; of these many were mere clusters of small houses far apart from similar congeries, and were cut off from one another by dense forests and imperfect roads. There was in the country no police force as we understand it now; but little, if any, organized local protection. Such protection as nominally existed was in the King or the great nobles who up to Wolsey's time held courts of their own and, under feudal tenure, controlled troops. The change of Sumptuary laws made by Wolsey, for the purpose of furthering trade and in order to bring the nobles round the King, had the effect of enlarging the groups of houses from villages to towns and cities. Up to that time the Sumptuary laws were prohibitive and repressive: what individuals and classes might *not* do or wear, rather than helpful to trade and manufacture; but under his clever statesmanship – exercised mainly on behalf of the King – the nature of these laws changed and trade and manufactures increased. But for a long, long time villages and towns were practically far apart; and in the wide spaces between the smaller communities were still under the old conditions.

Whilst this state of things existed, it was vitally necessary that wandering persons – who being without home were not easily made responsible – should be under some overt restraint, or at any rate, suspicion. The very word finally applied to such persons in the Acts of Parliament is in itself illuminative.

The first Vagrant statute recorded is that in the XXIII year of Edward III (1349). It runs as follows:

'Item because that many valiaunt beggers, as longe as thei maie live of begginge, do refuse to labour, gevinge them selfe to idlenes and vice, and sometyme to thefte and other abominations: None upon the saide peine of imprisonmente shall, under the colour of pitee or almes geve any thinge to suche, which male labour, or presume to favour them towards their desyres, so that therby thei maie be compelled to labour for their necessary lyvinge. Wherfore our saide Soveraine lorde the Kynge, the xiii daie of June, the xxiii yere of his reigne, hath commanded to all the shiryffes of Englande by divers writtes, that thei shall do openly to be proclaimed and holden, all and singular the premisses in the counties, boroughs, marchaunt townes, sea portes, and other places in their bailywekes, where to them shall seme expedient: And that thei do therof due execucion, as afore is saide.'

This Statute XXIII Edward III was called the 'Statute of Labourers' and was ordained to enforce the necessary labour required, 'because a great part of the people, and especially of workemen and servauntes late died in pestilence.' In this condition of things those remaining often refused to work except at wages unknown in those ages of political economy. In fact, the whole purpose was directly to insure a sufficiency of labour, or, at any rate, to secure such as existed. By means of the carrying out of the statute there would be a sort of registry of labour – certainly of the rebellious side of it. Its practical force was to bind every worker to his own town or tything.

In the next session of Parliament XXV Edward III this Statute was re-enacted, but with greater detail.

This purpose was still further maintained in a later Act – XXXIV Edward III, Cap. 1 – wherein power was given to arrest and imprison labourers unwilling to work as well as all guilty or even suspected persons and such Englishmen as 'have been pillours and robbers in the partyes beyond the sea; and be now come agayne and goeth wanderynge and will not labour as they were wonte in times past.'

Herein we get an idea of the cause for such rigid enactments regarding 'vagrom men' – to use Dogberry's phrase. Small communities were at times easily terrorized. The cities and towns had sheriffs and bailiffs and constables; but villages having no such official force at command could be easily 'held up' by a few men with cross-bows. There had, indeed, been cases on the Continent of Europe where towns had been attacked and sacked by masses of disbanded soldiery. Indeed, wanderers of every kind were harmful; for very often they were thieves or 'roberdsmen' or 'drawlatches'; and even if they did not commit heinous crimes they were a source of uneasiness and possible loss.

As yet in the history of British legislation, Parliament had only taken note of beggars and rebels against work at statute wage; but in the seventh year of the reign of Richard II an Act (Cap. 5) was passed in which amongst other things is the following:

'And moreover it is ordayned and assented to refrayn the malyce of dyvers people, faytours and wandrynge from place to place reumynge in the countrey more habundauntlie than they were wonte in tymes paste, that from hence forth the Justices of Assyses in theyre cessions the Justices of peace and the shyriffes in every countie shall have power to enquyre of all suche vacabundes and faytours and of theyre offences, and upon them to do that the lawe demaundeth. And that as well the iustices and shyryffes, as the mayres, baylyffes, constables and other governours of townes and places where such faytours and vacabundes shall come, shall from henceforthe have power to examyne them diligently and compell them to fynde suretye of theyr good bearynge by sufficyent mainpernours, of such as be distreynable, if any defaulte be founde in suche faytours and vacabundes. And if they can not fynde suche suretye they shall be sent to the next iayle, there to abyde tyll the Commynge of the iustices assygned for the deliverance of the iayles, who in suche case shal have power to do upon such faytours and vacabundes so imprisoned that that thereof to them best shall seme by the lawe.'

In the above enactment the word 'vacabunde' is mentioned for the first time. It is taken from the French through the low Latin word *vagari* – to wander; wandering beyond bounds. The previous enactments had compelled every man to remain in his own place; this one made the wandering itself from it an offence. We shall see how as time went on this was modified or intensified.

Five years later, by XII Richard II, Cap. 7, the rule against wandering was made more severe.

'Item it is accorded and assented, that of every persone that goeth begging, and is able to serve or labour, it shal be doen of him, as of him that departeth out of the Hundred, and other places aforesaid, without letter, testimonial, as afore is said, excepte people of Religion and Heremites, having letters testimoniall of their ordinaries, and that the beggars impotet [impoteut] to serve, shall abide in the cities and tounes, where they bee dwelling at the time of the proclamacion of this statute, and if the people of Cities or tounes, will not, or maie not suffice to finde theim: that then the saied beggars shall drawe them to other tounes within the Hundredes, Rape, or Wapentake, or to the tounes where thei were borne, within XL daies after the proclamacion made, and there shall continually abide, durying their lives, and that of all them that go in pilgrimage as beggars, and he able to travaille, it shall be doen as if the said servauntes and labourers, if thei have no letters testimoniall of their pilgrimage, under the saied seales. And that the scolers of the Universities that go so begging, have letters testimoniall of their Chaunceler, upon the same pein.'

The Act XI Henry VII, Cap. 2, is intended to be merciful and to spare undue cost to the public. By it 'vacaboundes,' instead of being put in jail, are to be given several chances of reformation:

'that the shyryffes, mayres, bayliffes, highe constables, and pety constables, and all other officers of cities, boroughes townes, townshyppes, vyllages and other places, within three daies after this Act proclaymed, make due serche, and take or cause to be taken all such, vacaboundes ydle and suspecte persones, lyvyng suspiciously, and them so taken to set in stockes, there to remayne by the space of thre daies and thre nightes and there to have none other sustenance but breade and water. And after the saide thre daies and thre nightes, to be had out and set at large, and then to be commaunded to avoide the towne. If the misdoer "eftsones" be taken in "suche defaute in the same town or township he is to be set in the stocks for six days on the same diet; and every one giving him meat or drink or favouring in his misdoing is to be fined in each time to pay a penalty of twelve pence".'

And also it is ordained by the same authorities that:

'all maner of begers, not able to work, within six wekes next after the proclamacion of this act, go, rest, and abide in that hundred where last he last dwelled, or there where he is best knowen or borne there to remaine and abyde without beggyne out of the saide hundred, upon peine to be punished as is aforesaide.'

Then it goes on that no man is to be excused by being a 'clerke of one universitee or the other,' unless he show letters from the Chancellor of that University; nor is one calling himself a soldier, shipman or travelling man unless he bring a letter from his captain or from the town where he landed 'and that he then to be commanded to go the straight high waie into his countrey.' If any sheriff or other officer omit to discharge this duty with regard to strangers he is to be fined for each case twenty pence. This regulation is protected by giving the Lord of the Manor or the Alderman of the ward a personal interest in such fines and to secure his reward by distraint. The last clause of the Act runs:

'Provided alwaie that diminucion of punishment of vacaboundes and beggers aforesaide, may and shall be had for women great with

chylde, and men and women in extreme sicknes, by him that hath auc-
toritee to doe the sayde punishments, this acte notwithstandynge.'

By an Act of eight years later (XIX Henry VII, Cap. 12) the severity
of punishment for first offence in vagabondage was reduced to one
day and night in the stocks on bread and water; and for a second
offence to three days and nights of similar durance. The same penalties are to be enforced on officers neglecting their duties under this Act
as in the earlier enactment.

In the first year of Edward VI an Act (1 Edward VI, Cap. 3) was
passed repealing all former Acts relating to vagabonds. This Act was
in turn repealed by another passed in the third year of the same King
(III Edward VI, Cap. 16). In the same year another similar Act was
passed which was in turn repealed by XIV Elizabeth, Cap. 5. There
were other temporary Acts of the time of Edward VI, Queen Mary and
Philip and Mary; also Acts I Elizabeth, Cap. 19, and V Elizabeth, Cap.
19. All of these were repealed by XIV Elizabeth, Cap. 5, which was the
most elaborate and comprehensive Vagabond Act passed by the
British Parliament up to that time, 1572.

This Act of 1572 is much too long to quote, but a survey of its provisions can be interesting. The preamble gives the necessity of its
enactment:

'Whereas the parts of this realme of England and Wales be
presentlie with roges, vagabonds, and sturdie beggers, exceedinglie
pestred, by meanes whereof daylie happen murders, thefts, and other
great outrages, to the high displeasure of Almightie God, and to the
great annoy of the common wealth,' etc.

Then came the provisions. All persons above the age of fourteen
who were in the class of 'roges, vagabonds or sturdie beggers' caught
begging, vagrant or misordering themselves were to be put in prison
and kept there without bail till the next coming sessions. Such persons,
being convicted, 'he or she shal be adiudged to be grievouslie
whipped and burnt through the gristle of the right eare, with a hot
yron of the compasse of an inch about, manifested his or her rogish
kind of life, and his or her punishment received for the same, whereof
entrie shall bee made of records by the clerke of the peace in the same
shire, in the recordes of the same sessions, which iudgement shall also
presentlie be executed, except some honest person' (here is stated the
property qualification of such) 'will of his charitie be contented to take
such offendour ... into his service for one whole yeere.' Such employ-
er is to be under recognizance to carry out the obligation thus undertaken. And if such offender abscond before the year is out he or she
'shall be whipped and burnt thorow the gristle of the right eare with a

hot yron, as is aforesaide.' Fourteen days' grace are to be allowed to the offender if sanctioned by two justices. Then if the offender fall again within three weeks into the same way of life if he or she be of or over eighteen years of age shall be adjudged a felon and suffer the penalties of such unless some honest person give recognizance (of double the former amount) to keep him or her in his service for two whole years. If the person thus taking service abscond a second time, then 'such roge or vagabond shall be taken, adiuged and deemed as a felon in all respectes, and shall in all degrees have, suffer and forfeite as a felon, without allowance or benefite of clergie or sancturie.'

'And if such roge or vagabond after fortie dayes next after he or she shall be two severall times taken into service as is aforesaide, doe either in the sayde Countie, or else where eftsoones the third time fall againe to a kind of rogish or vagabond trade of life: that then such roge or vagabond shall be adjudged and deemed for a felon, and suffer the paynes of death, and losse of landes and goods as a felon, without allowance or benefite of clergie or sanctuarie.'

The stringency of this Act is fortified by laying heavy penalties on any person harbouring or aiding a rogue or vagabond 'marked or not marked' travelling without a license from the justices; and by heavily punishing negligent constables.

There are in the Act some clauses of thoughtful benevolence. Certain travelling persons, shipmen, soldiers having licenses, are exempt. So also the following: 'any cockers or harvest folks ... either corne harvest, or hay harvest, if they do worke and labour accordinglie, neither yet to any that happeneth to be robbed or spoyled by ye way'; nor serving-men turned away or who have lost master or mistress by death. The Lord Chancellor's license is to go everywhere. Young persons under the age of fourteen are exempt from all consequences – except whipping or stocking – as by former Acts. Hospitals are empowered to harbour and help aged and impotent persons. Certain 'abyding places' are to be appointed locally in every shire, etc., in which the poor are to live and be provided for; but any poor person refusing to live in such place is to be deemed a rogue for the first refusal, and for the second to 'suffer as a roge or vagabond in the last degree of punishment set forth by this acte in all points.' The same punishment is to be meted to 'aged and impotent persons, not being so diseased lame or impotent, but that they may worke in some manner of worke' who refuse to do such work as the overseers appoint them to.

There is a special clause to the effect that in case of 'any begger's childe,' being above the age of five years and under fourteen years, being male or female, 'who may be liked of by any subject of this realme of honest calling,' such may be taken by them into service. This must be done under bond, and the master is bound to keep them till a stated age – twenty-four in the case of a male and eighteen in the case of a female.

This statute was the mother statute of many vagabond Acts or portions of Acts which lasted down to 1822 and became in certain ways the guiding legislation in the establishment of poors' houses and reformatories. Of course as time went on and social conditions changed the provisions had to be altered. As towns multiplied, bringing more constant and easier communication from place to place, the mere fact of being an unlicensed traveller ceased to be in itself an offence. In a populous country with much trade and many manufactures and industries it would be quite impossible to 'keep tab' of all vagrants. But till this day those who will not work are practically regarded as a more or less dangerous class. Indeed, the passing of the 'habitual criminals' Act has a common basis. When certain persons – or classes of persons – are manifestly dangerous to more peaceful and better-ordered classes of communities it is the essence of good government – indeed, a necessary duty to responsible officials – to keep them in restraint, or certainly under observation. In both civil and rural communities they are dangerous; in America as in England; to-day as well as in the time of 'Good Queen Bess.' In cities they are practically rogues; in the country vagabonds and sturdy beggars, whose presence is attended with fear if not with danger.

'It is the germ of the future which we seek in the past' – to use the luminous phrase of Victor Cousin. Why not apply this historical lesson to existing conditions? The reign of Queen Elizabeth was an enlightened time; and benevolent and tolerant ideas did not lack. If then the statesmen of that expansive and formative period found it necessary to rule tramps with so heavy a hand that cumulative penalties beginning with 'ear-marking' – which was the name applied to the branding in the ear – and ending with the extremist possible punishment, death, were ordained, why might it not be wise to adopt some drastic measure, though one necessarily more in accord with the humanitarian development of three centuries? If it was found necessary in the earlier period to put on the ill-doer some mark of which he could not divest himself, why should we not repeat the custom in some fashion in accord with the spirit of the times? If it was then found necessary to keep tramps within districts where they were personally known to officials, why not now keep them within certain bounds? If it was worth while then to try to break them in to the practice or habit of labour, why not repeat the benevolent enterprise?

For it is necessary to accustom the long-idle to labour by gentle exercise. The muscle, almost atrophied by disuse, cannot all at once either adapt themselves to or continue in strenuous work. I remember some years ago making a round of the police 'shelters' in New York; those most thoughtful refuges for the not, or not-yet, criminal poor. Two rooms, one for either sex; well warmed and furnished, with only plank beds and a can of cold water and tin cup. The weather was dreadfully cold, and that night the various shelters must have saved many lives. In one station the kind-hearted old sergeant of police took me into both rooms. It was a lesson to remember. In either room were as many persons as could find resting-place. Almost all of them had taken off all their poor rags, which they had hung to dry on lines stretched from wall to wall overhead. The smell of them was noisome. I had been talking to the sergeant of the possibility of reforming tramps and getting them to work. In the men's room he said to me:

'That will bear out what I told you, sir. Look at that man's muscles. He *can't* work. Not all at once, at any rate. His legs are all right, for he uses them. But mind his arms! Why, they're like those of a child of twelve. It would take him a couple of months, beginning easy, before he could use a spade, or chop wood!'

He was quite right. The man's arms were almost of skeleton leanness; and there was no rigour in the muscles at any moment.

In England the corresponding class to the American tramp is that of the 'bone-idle' who live nearly all their lives in the so-called workhouses. These men never work. When they are brought to book for refusing to work they go to gaol.

The time is fast coming when something *must* be done regarding the wilfully-idle class. Already in Germany if they refuse to work they must starve. The result is that they work enough to keep them from the latter alternative. In England the working classes are beginning to lose patience with the idle. The feeling has become more or less acute, now that a system of old-age pensions has come over the horizon. Naturally enough, the workers and earners are not satisfied with a scheme of pensioning at a certain age all who require it. They say that it is not fair that they who have lived honestly and worked hard – and in so doing have helped to gather the money required for the scheme of pensions – should be treated in the same way as the habitually-idle. Or they put it in a more reasonable form that the habitually-idle should not be given the same consideration as those habitually-industrious.

In America the class of 'tramp' is a perpetual menace; and that not merely to individuals. The lesson of the 'Coxey' army of tramps who gathered in thousands and made their way to Washington should not be forgotten. As they took their way the public on the route were so fearful of some excesses being committed that they bribed them with food and help to pass on from their own district. It was just such armies, only better equipped and trained to arms, which made the vagabond Acts from Edward III down a necessity of British Government.

How, then, could this historical lesson be applied?

If the 'tramp' of the twentieth century be so dangerous, or at best a source of fear or embarrassment – as was the 'Roge' or 'Vagabond' or 'Sturdie Beger' of the sixteenth; and as he was in the former age treated in such a way as to minimise his harmfulness, why not repeat the treatment, suitably altered to meet the new conditions! As ear-marking with a 'hot yron' be treatment of a drastic quality not acceptable to a less rude age, surely the resources of science are equal to some method of personal marking of an indelible quality. This step achieved, all idle persons, wandering and obviously undesirable to any ordinary intelligence, might in the first instance be arrested and tested as to the existence of modern ear-marking. If unable to show license or to account for themselves in any reasonable way they might be sent to a Labour Colony set far away in some fastness, there to be detained for a sufficient time to learn to be industrious in some form, and to have their physique brought by degrees up to the standard requisite for such work. It could be made apparent that there was no spirit of unkindness in such precautionary, and ultimately benevolent, doing.

The first relegation might be for a year; after which the reorganized tramp could, if considered to be physically unsuitable, be allowed to go free. Such would be in the routine of the old law. If a second time he were sent back to the labour colony he should have to pass two years in the service – again fulfilling the old conditions. By this time it would be known and proved whether he was simply a loafer or one who wished to do well. He had had his two chances and he could ask no more. The third period of duress would match the last stage in this eventful history. In this age we do not, and could not kill, because of mere idleness. But the offender could be given a life sentence. In England a life sentence really means twenty years. At the expiration of such times, if reformation were possible, it would be seriously undertaken now. If the intention of reform were not now apparent he could remain where he was – not dangerous, even if inefficient.